ZOE MINISTRIES INTERNATIONAL

HOW TO HEAR GOD'S VOICE
IN CHRIST

FACILITATOR MANUAL

Copyright © 1998, 2014 by ZOE Ministries International
All rights reserved.
Printed in the United States of America

This manual or parts thereof may not be reproduced, stored or transmitted in any form by any means without prior written permission of ZOE Ministries International, except as provided by United States of America copyright law.

ZOE Ministries International
PO Box 2207
Arvada CO 80001-2207, USA
permissions@zoemin.org

All scripture quotations, unless otherwise indicated, are taken from the Holy Bible, New International Version ® NIV ® Copyright © 1973, 1978, 1984 by Biblica, Inc.®. Used by permission of Zondervan. All rights reserved worldwide. www.zondervan.com

Scripture quotations marked (AMP) are taken from *The Amplified Bible, Old Testament.* Copyright © 1965, 1987 by The Zondervan Corporation. *The Amplified New Testament*, Copyright © 1954, 1959, 1987 by the Lockman Foundation. Used by permission.

Scripture quotations are taken from *The Message* Copyright © 1993 by Eugene H. Peterson. Used by permission of NavPress Publishing Group.

Some study note quotes taken from the HOLY BIBLE, NEW INTERNATIONAL VERSION ® NIV ®. Copyright © 1973, 1978, 1984, 2011 by Biblica, Inc. ®. Used by permission of Zondervan. All rights reserved worldwide. www.zondervan.com

Quotations from *The Full Life Study Bible*® (*now published as the Fire Bible® Global Study Edition*) used by permission of Life Publishers International, 1625 N Robberson Ave, Springfield, MO 65803, U.S.A., www.lifepublishers.org

Quotes used by permission from Finis Jennings Dake, Sr., Author of *Dake's Annotated Reference Bible.*

Some Scripture quotations in this publication are from *The New Kings James Version,* Copyright © 1979, 1980, 1982,1994 Thomas Nelson, Inc.
Excerpts taken from *The Holy Spirit Today* by Dick Iverson. Used by permission. © 1976 by Bible Temple.

Revision 01/20

WWW.ZOEMINISTRIES.ORG

ACKNOWLEDGMENTS

ZOE Ministries International is dedicated to training, equipping and sending believers into the world to minister by the leading of the Holy Spirit. This ministry helps build the body of Christ and encourages God's people to use their gifts and talents for His glory. It is for this purpose that this manual has been compiled by the leading of the Holy Spirit and the input of many people. ZOE Ministries wishes to thank them for their support, time and talents in putting this manual together. We give our Lord all the praise and glory for this work!

CONTENTS

Foreword		7
Introductory Comments to Facilitators		9
Lesson 1	Introduction	13
Lesson 2	Love and Unity	33
Lesson 3	Motive Gifts	45
Lesson 4	Motive Gifts—Perception and Serving	67
Lesson 5	Motive Gifts—Teaching and Exhortation	83
Lesson 6	Motive Gifts—Giving and Administration	99
Lesson 7	Compassion Motive Gift	113
Lesson 8	Getting Acquainted with the Holy Spirit	127
Lesson 9	The Intimacy of the Trinity	137
Lesson 10	Gifts of the Spirit—Revelation Gifts	165
Lesson 11	Gifts of the Spirit—Power Gifts	181
Lesson 12	Gifts of the Spirit—Vocal Gifts	195
Endnotes		213
Appendix A		221
Appendix B		223

This material is designed to be used within a specific format. Facilitator Training is a necessary prerequisite before this material may be used effectively in a Bible study or class setting.

ZOE MINISTRIES INTERNATIONAL

FOREWORD

Dear Facilitator,

We are so pleased that the Lord has led you to facilitate this course, How to Hear God's Voice—In Christ. We believe that this is one of our more exciting courses as you watch participants begin to understand themselves (and their mates, if married) and others in the body of Christ.

In this course you will examine the motive gifts discussed in Romans 12, along with the gifts of the Spirit mentioned in 1 Corinthians 12 and 14. However, to truly understand the operation of these gifts, you need to recognize and understand the person of the Holy Spirit in your life. Sandwiched between the study of the motive gifts and the gifts of the Spirit, the class will examine both the person of the Holy Spirit, as presented in John 14, 15 and 16, as well as the function of the Trinity as a whole.

You will be amazed as you watch God, through His Holy Spirit, reveal to the participants who they are in Christ. This is called discipleship!

May God bless you and your class in the next 12 weeks.

In His Love,

Dick and Ginny Chanda
Founding Directors

INTRODUCTORY COMMENTS
TO FACILITATORS

As an introduction to this manual, we have summarized information that we feel will be helpful to you during this course. Much of this information was covered during your facilitator training.

- DIRECTIONAL INFORMATION FOR FACILITATORS IS OUTLINED IN THIS FONT FOR QUICK IDENTIFICATION.

- In this How to Hear God's Voice—In Christ course, the facilitator will lead the Scripture discussions each week, with the exception of the motive gift Scripture passages assigned in Lessons 4 through 7. In those lessons, the facilitator should choose a participant who is strong in a specific gift to lead the Scripture discussion for that specific motive gift. If no one scores high in a specific motive gift, then the facilitator should lead that Scripture discussion. Participants should be asked to lead the book and assigned article discussions **beginning in Lesson 3.**

- **In Lessons 3 through 6, you will teach about specific motive gifts. After you teach on a specific motive gift, have participants fill out the questionnaires for that gift in class. The Scripture assignment for the following week will illustrate those specific gifts.**

- Remember, do not just teach this material unless you are instructed to do so in the manual. As a facilitator, you need to remember that you are a coach and you are there to encourage class participation.

- The first few lessons of this course will have a more instructional format. Some of the early lessons include teachings that provide a common base of understanding for your class members.

- If a lesson contains a teaching, please let the class know that you are teaching from the Facilitator Course Manual provided by ZOE Ministries International.

- Lessons 1 and 2 provide an opportunity for you to model how participants should lead class discussions later in the course.

- As a facilitator, it is your responsibility to encourage the class to share the insights that God gave them as they studied the assigned material. Ask questions that will draw out these insights.

- You are not expected, nor should you attempt, to cover every point in each lesson. These points are provided for your edification and only those that directly support the main principle should be included in the class discussion.

- As participants become more involved in leading class discussions, your primary purpose is to coordinate the class and allow the Lord to build individuals' confidence and leadership abilities.

- If during a class discussion someone's answer or insight is not quite right, please do not directly address this with the individual. Instead, redirect the discussion back to the main principle of the lesson.

- Remember, as a facilitator, you cannot solve each person's problems. You are to present principles from God's Word and allow the Holy Spirit to help class members apply them to their lives.

- Finally, we respectfully ask that this copyrighted material not be copied or reproduced for other purposes without express written permission from ZOE Ministries International. We request this not to control the material, but for two reasons:

  1) Without proper facilitator training, the class will not be what we feel the Holy Spirit wants it to be, and

  2) We need to honor those who have graciously given us permission to reprint or quote their materials. As stewards of their authorship, we are responsible for not using this material beyond the limitations that they have requested.

Thank you for your involvement in this ZOE course and we join you in praying that the Holy Spirit will transform participants' lives!

IN CHRIST

LESSON 1

INTRODUCTION

MAIN PRINCIPLE

God has fashioned each of us as a vessel for His use. As God's vessel, we contain His glory and the knowledge of Him. We should become the best vessel we can be and allow God's life and love to pour out of us to others.

LESSON 1

Introduction

I. Let's Get Started!

A. WELCOME THE CLASS.

B. OPEN WITH PRAYER.

C. GET ACQUAINTED. ASK PARTICIPANTS TO BRIEFLY SHARE SOMETHING ABOUT THEMSELVES, E.G., WHETHER THEY ARE MARRIED, HAVE CHILDREN, ETC. BEGIN BY SHARING ABOUT YOURSELF.

D. HAVE SOMEONE READ, THE MAIN PRINCIPLE FOR TODAY'S LESSON.

II. Introduction to ZOE Ministries International

A. The Purpose of ZOE Ministries

Zoe is a Greek word for *life* found in many Scriptures, including **John 17:3—"Now this is eternal life: that they may know you, the only true God, and Jesus Christ, whom you have sent."** The purpose of ZOE Ministries is to bring forth *zoe*, God's vibrant life, in individual believers so that their daily lives glorify God as they minister that life to others.

B. The Goal of ZOE Ministries

1. Our goal is to train and equip believers to make disciples, which is in keeping with the

commission given to us by Jesus in **Matthew 28:19–20**—"Therefore go and make disciples of all nations, baptizing them in the name of the Father and of the Son and of the Holy Spirit, and teaching them to obey everything I have commanded you. And surely I am with you always, to the very end of the age."

2. How do we accomplish our goal of making disciples?

   a. **By training and equipping through our courses**

      - **Hearing, Knowing, and Following God's Voice Courses**—This series of 12-week discipleship classes can help us hear God's voice in various aspects of Christian life. They provide discipleship in a group setting.

      - **Discipleship by the Word of God and the Power of the Holy Spirit**—This course provides training on how to disciple individuals one-on-one, thereby allowing them to take great strides in their personal relationship with God and in ministry. This method of discipleship uses the Word and the leading of the Holy Spirit as the only tools. It is changing lives in a very simple, yet powerful way.

      - **Captivated by Their Character**—To meet the need for evangelistic outreach, we have designed a home-based series of lessons. This three-part series is designed for the

unbeliever, new believer, or those who need a refresher on the Trinity. The six-week courses are:
1. Who Is Jesus?
2. Who Is the Father?
3. Who Is the Holy Spirit?

b. **By imparting God's life**
Our mission is to impart God's life (*zoe*) into the hearts of responsive people. We desire to see that *zoe* life manifested in individual believers, so that their daily lives glorify God as they minister that life to others.

c. **By connecting the Bride of Christ (the Church) with the Bridegroom**
Our heart is to see a holy, Spirit-led bride become alive with a burning passion for our soon-coming King, Judge and Bridegroom. God has called us to do this by training the bride (the Church) to hear, know and follow God's voice.

IF AVAILABLE, PLEASE DISTRIBUTE ZOE MINISTRIES INTERNATIONAL BROCHURES TO THOSE INTERESTED IN MORE INFORMATION OR REFER THEM TO THE ZOE WEBSITE: WWW.ZOEMINISTRIES.ORG.

III. Time of Worship
(DECIDE WHETHER YOUR CLASS SHOULD TAKE TIME TO WORSHIP DURING THIS LESSON.) SHARE THE FOLLOWING WITH THE CLASS, AS THE LORD LEADS:

There are several reasons why we take class time to worship.

Besides the fact that He is worthy of our praise, worship prepares our hearts to better hear God during class. It helps us get our eyes off of ourselves and back on the Lord. Worship reminds us of God's love, faithfulness and awesome power.

IV. Walking in Unity

Part of the task of discipleship is showing Christians how they can work together in unity with other believers.

- **A.** In the **Hearing God's Voice** course we looked at how to individually hear God's voice. In this course we consider how to corporately hear God's voice, as the body of Christ.

- **B.** We see too many examples of disunity in the body of Christ. We see individual believers or churches competing with one another. One purpose of this course is to enable believers to appreciate others in the body of Christ rather than walking in envy, resentment or strife. Our desire is to see the body of Christ functioning together the way God planned!

- **C.** When we misunderstand the Holy Spirit by seeing Him only as the "Giver of gifts," we fail to fully recognize and honor Him as a Person in the Trinity. It is He who transforms us into the likeness of Christ. It is He who enables us to minister effectively to one another. In this course, we will get to know the Holy Spirit better and learn how we can cooperate with Him.

- **D.** READ **JOHN 17:20–23.**

1. Unity is strongly emphasized in this passage. Here unity is already a given—not something to work toward. **Verse 21 says, "that all of them may be one, Father, just as you are in me and I am in you."** The verb tense of *be* in this verse connotes "that they may *continually be* one" rather than "that they become one."[1]

   And this unity that we have is like that of the Father and the Son. We have this unity because we have the Holy Spirit!

2. In this passage we also read about *glory*—the glory that the Father gave Jesus. *Thayer's Greek-English Lexicon of the New Testament* defines glory as preeminence, majesty, radiance and absolute perfection.[2] While Jesus was on earth, He was the radiance of God's glory, its exact representation (**Hebrews 1:3**)

   John 17:22 says that Jesus has given us this glory. Because Christ lives in us, we should reflect Christ's glory; people should be recognizing Jesus in us. We need to be vessels that God can use to draw people to Himself as they see His moral beauty, His radiance shining through us.

E. Walking in unity with each other reveals God's glory. However, until we know who we are as individuals in Christ, how God has created us and for what purpose, it is very difficult to walk in unity with our brothers and sisters in the Lord.

Lesson 1 — Introduction

> When we learn who we are and how God intends us to operate, we will complement each other, not compete with each other. When the Holy Spirit is allowed to minister through us in an orderly way, showing respect for each person, there will be greater unity in the body of Christ.

When we learn who we are in Christ, God's glory is reflected in us. Then we fulfill Jesus' prayer in **John 17:21—"May they also be in us so that the world may believe that you have sent me."**

F. In this course we will examine who we are in Christ, how God has created us, and how—by His Spirit—He plans to use us to extend His kingdom. We are His vessels—to be used for His glory!

V. What does it mean to be a vessel for God?

A. In **Acts 9:15** God told Ananias to go to Saul, saying, **"Go! This man is my chosen instrument to carry my name before the Gentiles and their kings and before the people of Israel."** In the *King James Version* it says, **"my chosen vessel."**

　　1. The word *chosen* carries the meaning of selected for oneself.

　　2. A *vessel* is an instrument by which something is done. It can be a container for substances including liquids. It can refer to a servant of God.[3]

3. The vessels used by Hebrew people were usually earthenware. This pottery was used to carry or store everything from documents to grain, wine or oil.

4. *The NIV Study Bible* states, "It was customary to conceal treasure in clay jars, which had little value or beauty and did not attract attention to themselves and their precious contents…"[4]

B. What a great picture this provides for the truths found in **2 Corinthians 4:6–7**. HAVE SOMEONE READ THESE VERSES ALOUD.

1. *The NIV Study Bible's* footnote for **verse 6** says, "The light that now shines in Paul's heart (qualifying him to be a proclaimer of Christ) is the knowledge of the glory of God as it was displayed in the face of Christ—who has come, not just from an earthly tabernacle, but from the glorious presence of God in heaven itself (see Jn 1:14)."[5]

2. READ **2 CORINTHIANS 4:6–7** IN *THE MESSAGE:*

> **Remember, our Message is not about ourselves; we're proclaiming Jesus Christ, the Master. All we are is messengers, errand runners from Jesus to you. It started when God said, "Light up the darkness!" and our lives filled up with light as we saw and understood God in the face of Christ, all bright and beautiful.**
>
> **If you only look at us, you might well miss the brightness. We carry this precious**

Message around in the unadorned clay pots of our ordinary lives. That's to prevent anyone from confusing God's incomparable power with us. As it is, there's not much chance of that.

VI. Steps in Being Created and Used as God's Vessel

We are vessels of God, carrying in us something very valuable—the knowledge of God's identity and character—in order to be able to give it to others.

A. Becoming Clay in the Master's Hands

1. **Isaiah 64:8** says, **"Yet, O Lord, you are our Father. We are the clay, you are the potter; we are all the work of your hand."**

    As a potter forms the pot with his hands, molding it into a beautiful, valuable vessel, so we, when submitted to the Master Potter's hands, will take on His beauty and His value!

2. The potter begins with a cold lump of clay. This represents what we are like before we are born again. When we accept Jesus as our Lord, God takes us into His hands and begins shaping us into the person He wants us to be. During the reshaping process He adds water to make the clay pliable, much like the influence of the Holy Spirit who indwells us at our rebirth.

B. Molding the Clay

READ **JEREMIAH 18:1–6**. This word from God came to the nation of Israel, but it can also be applied to us.

1. Verse **4** says, **"So the potter formed it into another pot, shaping it as seemed best to him."** How we are shaped is totally up to God.

2. If we are not turning out right, we may be heading toward a major reshaping.

3. SAY, "There are Christians who choose not to allow God to mold their lives. Why do you think this happens?"

We, like the clay, must be warmed by God's love and His presence in our lives. As He kneads us and works with us, we are shaped by Him. He endows us with giftings and abilities that can be used to build up the Church and to reach out to the lost.

C. Making the Vessel

1. After the clay is molded into its intended shape, it is set aside to dry. The potter watches to see if it will retain its shape.

    This can be likened to "dry" times in our walk with the Lord, when we may not overtly sense His presence. He watches to see if we will continue to be obedient to Him and will look to Him for what we need **(Deuteronomy 8:2)**.

2. Once the clay is dry, the potter may put a glaze on

it. The vessel is then placed in an oven, or kiln, and it is subjected to extreme heat. This firing is what makes the vessel strong and useful.

    a. READ **JOHN 6:60–66.** Often Christians find it too difficult to go through the fire—those tough times when things get really uncomfortable. Even some of Jesus' disciples, upon hearing Him teach, found it too difficult to continue following Him.

    b. When it gets tough to obey the Lord, we must not give up. This is a time of purification that prepares us for ministry. A pot that has not been glazed and fired will not hold water.

    c. READ **MATTHEW 3:11–12.**

3. Once we have been formed and fired by the Lord, it is easy to see that we Christians are not all alike.

If we allow God to apply the heat—the purifying fire of the Holy Spirit—we will be of greater service to Him.

---

    a. Sometimes we compare ourselves with other vessels of God and wish we could be more like them. However, God needs us all. He has fashioned each one of us for His own plans and purposes. We need to accept this fact. Many Christians do not know who they are in Christ and how Christ operates in their lives. This lack of understanding can cause them to be discontented with themselves.

b. HAVE SOMEONE READ **ROMANS 9:20–21.**

c. READ THESE SAME VERSES FROM *THE MESSAGE* BELOW.

> "Who in the world do you think you are to second-guess God? Do you for a moment suppose any of us knows enough to call God into question? Clay doesn't talk back to the fingers that mold it, saying, 'Why did you shape me like this?' Isn't it obvious that a potter has a perfect right to shape one lump of clay into a vase for holding flowers and another into a pot for cooking beans?"

D. Using the Vessel

1. During this course we will discover exactly how we, as God's vessels, can most effectively be used by Him. In the first half of this training course we will identify our in-born motive gifts. We'll begin to see what kind of a vessel God has created us to be. Identifying and understanding our natural gifting, our motive gifts, will help us serve God more effectively. Understanding the motive gifts of the people with whom we work and live can greatly enhance our relationships with them and can help us all walk in unity. These motive gifts, which are found in **Romans 12,** will be discussed by looking at examples of people in Scripture who operated in the different motive gifts.

   In the second half of this course we will examine the Person of the Holy Spirit—who He is and what He does. By looking at **1 Corinthians 12** and **14** we will see how His gifts can manifest in us to support

Lesson 1 — Introduction

and build up of the body of Christ.

2. In order to be of use to God, we need to have the Holy Spirit poured out on us and to be reborn. READ **TITUS 3:4–6.** The Holy Spirit is responsible for our washing, rebirth and renewal. He was generously poured out on us through Jesus Christ.

In order to be of greatest use to God, we need to ask ourselves the following questions: "Is the living water within me going out to other people or is it held back like a dam?" and "Am I allowing the Holy Spirit to use me as His vessel so that His life pours out of me to benefit others?"

3. **HAVE SOMEONE READ JOHN 7:37–39.**

   a. A practical illustration of this dynamic involves a farmer using a siphon tube to water his cornfield. He does this by placing one end of the siphon tube into an irrigation ditch filled with water and placing the other end on the ground. As the farmer puts the siphon tube in the irrigation ditch, water gushes out the other end. He can watch the heads of the corn pop up as they are refreshed by the water.
   We need to act as siphon tubes bringing water to the parched land. As we spend time with one hand immersed in the water—which is God's Word and the presence of the Lord—the Holy Spirit will cause His living water to bubble up out of us and flow through us to people in need.

    b. As the water gushes out of the siphon tube, the farmer also sees rodents and other harmful animals flee from the water. This water is like the power of God and the authority we have in Christ to minister to people. His authority and power causes demons to flee, changing peoples' lives. We must have rivers flowing out continuously in order to minister like that. This means we need to spend time immersing ourselves in the water—in the Word and in God's presence.

4. In order to be used by God as honorable vessels we need to be cleansed. READ **2 TIMOTHY 2:20–22**.

   Verse 21 in *The Amplified Bible* **reads, "So whoever cleanses himself [from what is ignoble and unclean, who separates himself from contact with contamination and corrupting influences] will [then himself] be a VESSEL set apart and useful for honorable and noble purposes, consecrated and profitable to the Master, fit and ready for any good work" (AMP).**

E. **Conclusion**

The reason we are made to be God's chosen vessels is so that we can generously love. Let's end this discussion by reading **John 17:20–26**.

"My prayer is not for them alone. I pray also for those who will believe in me through their message, *that all of them may be one, Father, just as you are in me and I am in you. May they also be in us so that the*

Lesson 1 — Introduction

world may believe that you have sent me. I have given them the glory that you gave me, that they may be one as we are one: I in them and you in me. May they be brought to complete unity to let the world know that you sent me and have loved them even as you have loved me.

"Father, I want those you have given me to be with me where I am, and to see my glory, the glory you have given me because you loved me before the creation of the world.

"Righteous Father, though the world does not know you, I know you, and they know that you have sent me. *I have made you known to them, and will continue to make you known in order that the love you have for me may be in them and that I myself may be in them.*"

LEAD A PRAYER FROM THE VERSES ITALICIZED ABOVE.

Let us join our hearts in prayer and ask the Lord to bring unity to the Body of Christ, that we may be one as the Father and Son are one.

VII. Discussion of the Class Articles

TIME PERMITTING, HAVE CLASS MEMBERS TAKE TURNS READING PORTIONS OF THESE ARTICLES ALOUD. IF ANYONE IS UNCOMFORTABLE READING ALOUD, HE MAY PASS AND NOT READ. ASK CLASS MEMBERS WHAT THEY THOUGHT WERE THE MOST IMPORTANT POINTS IN THESE ARTICLES.

VIII. Class Format—Lessons 2–12

A. Opening Time

This includes welcoming the class, prayer for that session, worshiping the Lord (unless in a shortened class), sharing what God has done in the previous week, and making announcements.

B. Discussion of the Book, Scripture and Articles

1. The reading assignments for each week are listed on the course outline in the Study Guide. MAKE SURE PARTICIPANTS UNDERSTAND WHAT THEY ARE SUPPOSED TO READ FOR LESSON 2, AND REVIEW THE MAIN PRINCIPLE FOR NEXT WEEK'S LESSON.

2. Everyone needs to come prepared to share what he learned, as the Lord leads.

3. The facilitator and assistant will lead the book, article and Scripture discussions through Lesson 2.

4. Beginning in Lesson 3, one participant will be asked to lead the book and the assigned article discussions. In this course a facilitator will usually lead the Scripture discussion.

5. We cannot emphasize enough the importance of everyone asking the Holy Spirit for new insights from the Scriptures.

C. Ministry Time
A ministry time will end each class.

D. Class Length

The length of the class is approximately 2–2½ hours (1½ hours for a shortened class).

IX. Your Responsibility as a Participant

REFER THE CLASS TO THE ARTICLE IN THEIR STUDY GUIDE ABOUT THE PARTICIPANT'S RESPONSIBILITIES. REVIEW THIS ARTICLE WITH THEM NOW.

In addition, class members should keep confidential everything that is shared during class.

X. Ministry Time

A. AS FACILITATOR, YOU NEED TO GUIDE THE MINISTRY TIME. REFER TO THE CLASS FORMAT SECTION OF THE *FACILITATOR TRAINING STUDY GUIDE* AND READ THE "MINISTRY TIME" SECTION. (Note: This *Facilitator Training Study Guide* is the book you received during Facilitator Training.)

B. DURING THE MINISTRY TIME, WE SUGGEST THAT YOU DO NOT ASK CLASS MEMBERS FOR THEIR PRAYER REQUESTS. SAY TO THE PARTICIPANTS, "In general, in this course we wait until Lesson 4 to begin personal prayer ministry. In Lesson 4 during the ministry time, we will begin praying for participants who have the motive gift discussed in that lesson."

C. ON THE OTHER HAND, IF YOU SENSE THE LORD DIRECTING YOU TO ADDRESS THE NEED FOR PERSONAL PRAYER MINISTRY IN A CLASS MEMBER, ASK THE PERSON CONCERNED IF HE WOULD LIKE PRAYER.

D. INITIALLY, YOU MAY NEED TO DO THE MINISTERING, THEREBY SETTING THE EXAMPLE FOR THE CLASS.

E. AT THE BEGINNING OF THE MINISTRY TIME REMIND PARTICIPANTS ABOUT THE FOLLOWING:

As we minister to each other, we need to recognize that we are all fine-tuning our hearing of God's voice. We may not hear clearly all the time, so we need to carefully weigh any word of prophecy a class member gives us. The following is a helpful guideline:

If it doesn't make sense, put it on the shelf. If it contradicts what God has told you, let it drop. If your spirit confirms it, make a note of it in your journal and watch God bring it about.

F. ENCOURAGE HANDS-ON MINISTRY BY CLASS MEMBERS. ALLOW THE GIFTS OF THE SPIRIT TO MANIFEST IN DIFFERENT PEOPLE.

G. BE CAREFUL THAT ONE PERSON DOES NOT DOMINATE THE MINISTERING.

H. CLOSE THE CLASS WITH PRAYER. A SAMPLE CLOSING PRAYER FOLLOWS:

"Father, we thank You for what You have done in our lives today. We ask that by Your Holy Spirit You would seal all that was accomplished. Bring clarity to our hearts regarding the way You have created each of us. As we comprehend who we are in Christ, may we recognize and respect the way You created others in the body. May we walk in unity and <u>be one as Jesus and the Father are one.</u> Make us vessels fit to fulfill Your purposes. Guard and protect us until we meet again, and give us insight about the readings assigned for next week. In Jesus' mighty name, Amen."

IN CHRIST

LESSON 2

LOVE AND UNITY

MAIN PRINCIPLE

God calls us to abide in Christ and live in love and unity with one another. As we do this, we will be witnesses of God's love to the world. As we have communion with the Holy Spirit, we allow Him to make us into the image of Christ Jesus and to hold us together in unity. Remember, Jesus is the true vine and we are the branches, but the Holy Spirit is the sap that brings life and causes us to bear fruit that remains!

WWW.ZOEMINISTRIES.ORG

LESSON 2

Love and Unity

I. Let's Get Started!

A. WELCOME THE CLASS AND ENCOURAGE PARTICIPANTS TO SHARE WHAT GOD HAS BEEN DOING IN THEIR LIVES THIS PAST WEEK.

B. OPEN WITH PRAYER.

C. WORSHIP THE LORD.

SHARE THE FOLLOWING WITH THE CLASS, AS THE LORD LEADS.

There are several reasons why we take class time to worship. Besides the fact that He is worthy of our praise, worship prepares our hearts to hear God better during class. It helps us get our eyes off of ourselves and back on the Lord. Worship reminds us of God's love, faithfulness and awesome power.

D. READ, OR HAVE SOMEONE READ, THE MAIN PRINCIPLE FOR TODAY'S LESSON.

Due to the large reading assignments in the second half of this course, we will begin reading Renner's book, *The Dynamic Duo*, at the beginning of the course. Even though this book may not seem related to the study of the motive gifts in Lessons 3 through 7, we need to keep in mind that it is the Holy Spirit living in us who perfects our gifting to His glory. We will begin looking at the Holy Spirit in His entirety beginning in Lesson 8. Meanwhile, Renner's book will prepare us for the last five weeks of the course.

Lesson 2 — Love and Unity

II. Supporting Principles From the Book

ASK THE HOLY SPIRIT TO GUIDE YOU TO THE PORTIONS OF THE BOOK ASSIGNMENT THAT ARE IMPORTANT FOR YOUR CLASS TO DISCUSS. THE MAIN PRINCIPLE FOR THE LESSON MAY AID YOU IN FINDING THE IMPORTANT POINTS.

III. Supporting Principles From Scripture—
Ephesians 4:3
John 15:1–17

  A. Ephesians 4:3
"Make every effort to keep the unity of the Spirit through the bond of peace."

    1. Ask participants what insights the Lord gave them regarding this verse.

    2. The following quote comes from a footnote in the *Full Life Study Bible*.

> "The unity of the Spirit" cannot be created by any human being. It already exists for those who have believed the truth and received Christ as the apostle proclaimed in chs. 1–3. The Ephesians are now to keep that unity, not through human efforts or organizations, but by living "a life worthy of the calling [they] have received" (v. 1). Spiritual unity is maintained by being loyal to the truth and by keeping in step with the Spirit (vv. 1–3, 14, 15; Gal 5:22–26). It cannot be attained "by human effort" (Gal 3:3). [1]

B. John 15:1–3

1. In order for God's love to prevail in us and in order for us to successfully live in unity, we need to abide in Christ.

    a. Jesus is our example of obedience to the Father, being fruitful and glorifying the Father. He is the **"true vine" (verse 1)**.

    b. "The vine is frequently used in the OT as a symbol of Israel…When this imagery is used, Israel is often shown as lacking in some way. Jesus, however, is the 'true vine.' "[2] He is faithful and is not lacking in His ability to love the Father.

2. God the Father is the gardener.

    a. If we don't bear fruit, He will cut us off.

        What does it mean to bear fruit?

        The NIV Study Bible comments in a footnote: "In the NT the figure of good fruit represents the product of a godly life (see Mt 3:8; 7:16–20) or virtues of character (see Gal 5:22–23; Eph 5:9; Php 1:11).[3] As the world sees this kind of fruit, people will be drawn to God.

        If our hearts resist God's work to encourage holiness in us to make us holy, we will be cut off from the vine—removed from intimate fellowship with God and believers. We see an example of this in **John 6:60–66**, when some of the disciples of Jesus left Him because His teachings were too hard to hear.

b. If we do bear fruit, He will prune us so that we will bear more fruit.

What does it mean to be pruned?
A vinedresser will prune a grapevine to increase its fruit production. He allows only so many buds on each cane, or branch, of the vine. Each branch is shortened so that the producing buds are closer to the vine's trunk.[4] We are the branches in this Scripture, and the vine's trunk would be Jesus (**verse 5**).

- Being pruned by the Father could mean being disciplined by Him when we stray off target. This discipline is a sign of His love for us (**Proverbs 3:12**).

- It could mean a time of cutting back our activities so that we are doing only those works to which God has called us, thereby providing more time to spend with Him.

c. A new grape vine is trained and pruned over three years in preparation for its maximum fruit production.[5] Jesus prepared His disciples during His three years of ministry on earth. At the end of that time they were very fruitful and were mightily used by God. During His time with them, Jesus continually taught them. His words to His disciples caused them to be "clean," as He forgave them, loved them, showed them how to live godly lives, and chastised them when they needed correction (**verses 2–3**).

C. John 15:4–17

1. The only way to bear fruit is to remain, or abide, in Jesus (**verses 4–6**). To *abide* is to lodge, to be still in (His) possession, to wait for, to maintain unbroken fellowship with.[6]

    a. Remaining in Jesus involves letting His words remain in us (**verse 7**). Jesus' words are imparted in Scripture as well as through what His Spirit tells us in prayer. Consequently, we must spend time daily reading and meditating on Scripture and applying it to our lives, as well as investing time talking and *listening* to Him in prayer. It also involves continually asking for the filling of the Holy Spirit and maintaining on-going fellowship with the Lord.

    b. As we abide in Jesus, we will walk as He walked, we will live as He taught by His example. **1 John 2:6** says, **"Whoever claims to live in Him must walk as Jesus did."**

    c. Remaining in Jesus requires keeping His commands (**verses 10, 14**). And, what He commands is *that we love one another* just as He has loved us—by laying down His life for us (**verses 12, 17**).

        - In this teaching Jesus is talking to believers. If we don't walk in love and unity with fellow believers, we are not abiding in Jesus! If we

Lesson 2 — Love and Unity

are not abiding in Jesus, we will not bear fruit!

- We need to realize and receive Jesus' love for us so that we can give out His love to others.

2. What are the results of remaining in Jesus?

   a. Remaining in Jesus makes our prayers effective (**verses 7, 16**). If Jesus' words remain in us and we do what Jesus tells us to do, we can speak His Word as we pray for individuals and God's power will be released to do great things in their lives.

TO HELP CLASS MEMBERS BETTER UNDERSTAND JESUS' STATEMENTS IN **VERSES 7** AND **16**, HAVE THEM TURN TO P. 106 OF RENNER'S BOOK *THE DYNAMIC DUO*. READ ALOUD RENNER'S EXPLANATION OF WHAT IT MEANS TO ABIDE IN JESUS AND TO HAVE HIS WORD ABIDE IN YOU.

   b. Remaining in Jesus enables us to bear much fruit (**verses 7–8**).

   c. When we bear His fruit, people will know that we are disciples of Jesus. Bearing fruit glorifies the Father (**verse 8**). As we live godly lives and walk in the power of the Holy Spirit, it gives the world a glimpse of what God is like.

   d. Abiding in Jesus allows Jesus' joy to be in us (**verse 11**). What a witness to the world! A life filled with joy regardless of circumstances is a rarity in today's stressful world.

As we "walk like Jesus walked," it gives the Lord great joy as He sees His ministry on earth continuing through us. We can experience His joy and excitement within us because His Spirit dwells in us.

e. Remaining in Jesus and doing what He commands makes us Jesus' friends. *This is a new relationship*—no longer are we just servants (a title which Paul was proud to claim) (**verse 14**).

- Now we are His friends. This is reminiscent of Moses who went into the Tent of Meeting. There **"the Lord would speak to Moses face to face, as a man speaks with his friend" Exodus 33:11.**

- Jesus is saying that because we are friends, He will let us in on His business and take us into His confidence (**verse 15**). Jesus did only what the Father told Him to do (**John 12:49; John 14:10, 31**). Just as the Father told Jesus to pray for specific people, and even what to say, through the Holy Spirit, the Father also directs us through the Holy Spirit so that we can participate in what God wants to do in *our* time and place.

- This new relationship with the Lord is one of trust—trust in us to bear lasting fruit and to share with the world the Good News about Christ.

Lesson 2 — Love and Unity

D. Summary

So, the Father is the gardener.
Jesus is the true vine.
We are the branches.
Where is the Holy Spirit in all this? He is the sap that flows from the Father, through the Son, and brings us life and causes us to grow.

IV. Discussion of the Assigned Articles

TIME PERMITTING, ASK CLASS MEMBERS WHAT THEY THOUGHT WERE THE MOST IMPORTANT POINTS IN THESE ARTICLES.

V. Next Week's Assignment

A. REVIEW NEXT WEEK'S ASSIGNMENT ON THE COURSE OUTLINE.

B. REVIEW THE MAIN PRINCIPLE FOR NEXT WEEK'S CLASS.

C. ASSIGN ONE CLASS MEMBER TO LEAD THE BOOK DISCUSSION AND ANOTHER FOR THE ASSIGNED ARTICLE DISCUSSION FOR LESSON 3. FACILITATORS SHOULD LEAD THE SCRIPTURE DISCUSSION.

NOTES TO THE FACILITATOR:
YOU NEED TO CALL OR VISIT THE LESSON 3 DISCUSSION LEADERS DURING THE WEEK BEFORE THE CLASS. SEE THE **APPENDIX** FOR QUESTIONS YOU CAN USE DURING THESE CONVERSATIONS TO HELP THE LEADERS

PREPARE FOR THIS CLASS. REMEMBER TO CALL THE DISCUSSION LEADERS DURING THE WEEK BEFORE *EACH* LESSON.

VI. Ministry Time

A. AS FACILITATOR, YOU NEED TO GUIDE THE MINISTRY TIME. REFER TO THE CLASS FORMAT SECTION OF THE *FACILITATOR TRAINING STUDY GUIDE* AND READ THE MINISTRY TIME SECTION. (Note: This *Facilitator Training Study Guide* is the book you received during Facilitator Training.)

B. DURING THE MINISTRY TIME, WE SUGGEST THAT YOU DO NOT ASK CLASS MEMBERS FOR THEIR PRAYER REQUESTS. SAY TO THE PARTICIPANTS, "In general, in this course we wait until Lesson 4 to begin personal prayer ministry. In Lesson 4 during the ministry time, we will begin praying for participants who have the motive gift discussed in that lesson."

C. ON THE OTHER HAND, IF YOU SENSE THE LORD DIRECTING YOU TO ADDRESS THE NEED FOR PERSONAL PRAYER MINISTRY IN A CLASS MEMBER, ASK THE PERSON CONCERNED IF HE WOULD LIKE PRAYER

D. INITIALLY, YOU MAY NEED TO DO THE MINISTERING, THEREBY SETTING THE EXAMPLE FOR THE CLASS.

E. AT THE BEGINNING OF THE MINISTRY TIME REMIND PARTICIPANTS ABOUT THE FOLLOWING:

As we minister to each other, we need to recognize that we are all fine-tuning our hearing of God's voice. We may not hear clearly all the time, so we need to carefully weigh any word of prophecy a class member gives us. The following is a helpful guideline:

If it doesn't make sense, put it on the shelf. If it contradicts what God has told you, let it drop. If your spirit confirms it, make a note of it in your journal and watch God bring it about.

F. ENCOURAGE HANDS-ON MINISTRY BY CLASS MEMBERS. ALLOW THE GIFTS OF THE SPIRIT TO MANIFEST IN DIFFERENT PEOPLE.

G. BE CAREFUL THAT ONE PERSON DOES NOT DOMINATE THE MINISTERING.

H. CLOSE THE CLASS WITH PRAYER. A SAMPLE CLOSING PRAYER FOLLOWS:

"Father, we thank You for what You have done in our lives today. We ask that by Your Holy Spirit You would seal all that was accomplished. Bring clarity to our hearts regarding the way You have created each of us. As we comprehend who we are in Christ, may we recognize and respect the way You created others in the body. May we walk in unity <u>and be one as Jesus and the Father are one</u>. Make us vessels fit to fulfill Your purposes. Guard and protect us until we meet again, and give us insight about the readings assigned for next week. In Jesus' mighty name, Amen."

IN CHRIST

LESSON 3

MOTIVE GIFTS

MAIN PRINCIPLE

God has given each of us in-born gifts that we should use to build up the body of Christ. Discovering how God has gifted each of us can promote unity because then we can better understand and help one another.

WWW.ZOEMINISTRIES.ORG

LESSON 3

Motive Gifts

I. Let's Get Started!

    A. WELCOME THE CLASS.

    B. OPEN WITH PRAYER.

    C. WORSHIP THE LORD.

    D. READ, OR HAVE SOMEONE READ, THE MAIN PRINCIPLE FOR TODAY'S LESSON.

NOTE: WATCH YOUR TIME DURING THE DISCUSSION SECTIONS SO THAT YOU HAVE SUFFICIENT TIME TO COVER THE TEACHING SECTIONS.

II. Supporting Principles From the Book

ENCOURAGE THE DISCUSSION LEADER AND PARTICIPANTS TO FOCUS ON PORTIONS OF THE BOOK ASSIGNMENT THAT ARE IMPORTANT FOR THIS CLASS TO DISCUSS, ESPECIALLY AS IT RELATES TO THE MAIN PRINCIPLE.

III. What Are Motive Gifts?

THE FOLLOWING SECTION SHOULD BE TAUGHT.

A. Motive Gifts

In order to understand motive gifts, we need to remember the difference between the seven motive gifts listed in **Romans 12** and the nine spiritual gifts listed in **1 Corinthians 12**.

The nine spiritual gifts listed in **1 Corinthians 12** are manifestations of the Holy Spirit that God enables or empowers through us. The Holy Spirit moves upon us with these spiritual gifts, and they come and go according to need. On the other hand, motive or motivational gifts found in **Romans 12** determine the way we *are* innately. God places these in us at conception.

1. Our motivational gifts are the things that naturally move us.

    a. Our motivational gifts are the real factors behind our decisions and actions. They explain why and how we do things. Our motive gifts undergird, influence and determine the way we behave, think and talk.

Our motivational gifts activate what we do naturally because God has placed them in us by virtue of creation. They inspire us to act and react without much thinking. It doesn't take a conscious effort for us to function as God has designed.

b. Our motive gifts are our base of operations 24 hours a day.

2. God wants to anoint our motivational gifts with His Spirit.

   a. Unless our motive gifts are yielded to God and His purposes, they could slip out of His perfect will and be used for selfish or prideful purposes.
   b. Totally surrendering them to the Lord allows Jesus' love, power and creativity to flow through us.

3. We need to depend on others to complement and balance our gifts.

   a. God takes everyone's different gifts and puts them together to create a greater strength!

   b. As we come to understand our own strengths and weaknesses, we more fully appreciate the other motive gifts. We realize our need for one another. We must depend on each other in order to complete the tasks God has given us.

THE FOLLOWING SECTION SHOULD BE A CLASS DISCUSSION.

B. Romans 12:1–8

In this chapter the apostle Paul instructs Christians in Rome about their duty toward God and their neighbors.

1. **Verse 1** tells us to present our bodies to God as **"living sacrifices."**

   a. In the Old Testament sacrificing to God required

a priest to kill an animal, cut it into pieces and place it on the altar.

b. Sacrifice was important, but even in the Old Testament, God made it clear that obedience from the heart was much more important (**1 Samuel 15:22**). The Lord wants us to offer ourselves as living sacrifices—daily laying aside our own desires to follow Him.

c. A footnote from *The NIV Study Bible* states that the term *living sacrifices* is "in contrast to dead animal sacrifices, or perhaps 'living' in the sense of having the new life of the Holy Spirit."[1]

2. **Verse 2 tells us to "be transformed by the renewing of your mind."**

   a. *Be transformed* is a passive verb; we do not transform ourselves. The Holy Spirit does the transforming as we present ourselves to God. *Transform* in Greek is *metamorphoo* (met-am-or-fo´-o), which is related to the English word *metamorphosis*. It means to change into another form, to change in moral character for the better, to be "transformed into the same image (of consummate excellence that shines in Christ)."[2]

   b. **Ephesians 4:22–23** echoes this passive verb tense. **"You were taught, with regard to your former way of life, . . . to be made new in the attitude of your minds . . . ."** We may cooperate with the Holy Spirit by spending time in God's Word, but just reading Scripture will not renew our minds. It is the Holy Spirit who transforms us as we present ourselves to God as a spiritual act of worship.

3. We are given grace and faith by God to use these motivational gifts. In **verse 3** Paul says that he is writing this letter to the Corinthian church by the grace God has given him. We are also intended to use our motive gifts by God's grace, for God's purposes (**verses 3, 6**).

4. In **verse 5** we read that as believers, we are encouraged to see ourselves as members of **"one body."**

   a. This body is the Church, which has Jesus Christ as its head. **Ephesians 1:22–23 says, "And God placed all things under his feet and appointed him to be head over everything for the church, which is his body, the fullness of him who fills everything in every way."**

   As members of this body we have different functions, but we are coordinated by Jesus through the Holy Spirit.

   b. We belong to each other. Our motive gifts are to be shared with others in the body of Christ.

5. **Verses 6–8** discuss the different motive gifts: perception (prophecy), serving, teaching, exhortation, giving, administration and compassion (mercy).

THE FOLLOWING SECTION SHOULD BE TAUGHT. ASK PARTICIPANTS TO TURN TO THE CLASS ARTICLE **"THREE BIBLICAL GROUPS OF GIFTS."**

Lesson 3 — Motive Gifts

IN AN EFFORT TO BE CONCISE, WE WILL BE USING MALE PRONOUNS (LIKE "HE" AND "HIS") TO REFER TO BOTH MEN AND WOMEN.

IV. Three Biblical Groups of Gifts

A. The Ministry Gifts [The Five-Fold Ministry]

1. This gifting group is found in **Ephesians 4:7–16.** Let's turn there in our Bibles now and read these verses.

2. These gifts are given by Christ to people He has called into full-time service. Their gifts are given *to equip the saints until they reach unity and maturity* (**verses 12–13**). Each of these callings can be represented by one of the five fingers on your hand.

    a. The *apostle* is one who is sent.
    Position on the hand: The thumb—which can touch and work with all the other fingers.
    An apostle's ministry touches all the components of the five-fold ministry.
    Biblical example: Paul—**Galatians 1:1**

    An apostle is usually involved in planting new churches, where all of those gifts would be needed. This office or calling has remained relatively unoccupied in modern time. We will see more people move in this calling as the end time approaches.

    b. The *prophet* foretells the future. A true prophet's words are correct and his predictions come to pass.

Position on the hand: The pointer finger.
The prophet points to the future or to the past,
or calls people to repentance.
Biblical example: Agabus—**Acts 11:27–28**

c. The *evangelist* travels, proclaiming Christ.
Position on the hand: The middle finger.
The evangelist stands above the others as a soul winner. His words convict sinners and encourage believers.
Biblical example: Philip—**Acts 8:4–8, 26–40**

d. The *pastor* protects and oversees the church.
Position on the hand: The ring finger.
The pastor is "married" to his flock. He loves, feeds and, when necessary, corrects them.
Biblical example: Timothy—**1 and 2 Timothy**

e. The *teacher* clarifies truth for the church.
Position on the hand: The little finger.
The teacher brings balance to the rest of the five-fold ministry by teaching from the Scriptures.
Biblical examples: Priscilla and Aquila—**Acts 18:24–26**

B. The Spiritual (or Manifestation) Gifts

1. This group is discussed in **1 Corinthians 12** and **14**. Let's turn to **Corinthians 12:1–11** and read these verses.

2. These are supernatural gifts that are manifestations of the Holy Spirit as He moves upon believers. These gifts are administered by the Holy Spirit for

the common good, using whom He chooses, and at the time of need.

    a. Three *revelation* gifts: word of wisdom
                                                    word of knowledge
                                                    discerning of spirits

    b. Three *power* gifts: gift of faith
                                               gifts of healing
                                               working of miracles

    c. Three *spoken* gifts: prophecy
                                               speaking in tongues
                                               interpretation of tongues

C. The Motive Gifts

1. This group is found in **Romans 12:6–8**. Turn there now.

2. At conception, God places within each individual a motive gift, along with the faith to develop and use that gift.

3. The motive gifts are not like the *ministry gifts* which *Jesus gives*, to which some people *are called*. They are not like the *spiritual gifts* the *Holy Spirit manifests* as He *moves upon* a believer for a specific time and purpose. *Motive gifts* are *placed within by God* at conception, along with the faith to develop and use that gift

4. The term "motive gift" is not a scriptural word, but it describes the gift that moves out from your inner being. Your motive gift is what *motivates* you and interests you. It is the reason behind your actions. It helps to describe how you view things.

5. Motive gifts show our God-appointed positions in the body of Christ. Discovering your motive gift can help you more fully understand what God wants you to do.

6. Examining these gifts helps us better understand the God-appointed positions of others with whom we live and work. This can contribute to greater love and unity in marriage, in family, at work, with friends and at church.

7. Failure to understand the motivational gifts of other believers can lead to resentment and discord. Chuck Swindoll wrote the following illustration:

   We are like a pack of porcupines on a frigid, wintry night. The cold drives us closer together into a tight huddle to keep warm. As we begin to snuggle really close, our sharp quills cause us to jab and prick each other—a condition which forces us apart. But, before long we start getting cold, so we move back to get warm again, only to stab and puncture each other once more. And so, we participate in this strange, rhythmic tribal dance. We cannot deny it—we *need* each other, yet we *needle* each other.[3]

8. Jesus possessed all seven motive gifts. These seven gifts together depict the function of the body of Christ. They are *perception* (or *prophecy*), *serving*, *teaching*, *exhortation*, *giving*, *administration* and *compassion* (or *mercy*).

9. HAVE PARTICIPANTS TURN TO THEIR BOOKLET, **"DISCOVER YOUR GOD-GIVEN GIFTS."** READ ALOUD THE

Lesson 3 — Motive Gifts

MOTIVATIONAL GIFTS OVERVIEW.

10. While we may operate well in several of these areas, usually we are stronger in one of the motive gifts.

11. READ **1 PETER 4:10–11**. The purpose of these gifts is to serve others and glorify God.

D. 1 Corinthians 12:28–30

1. Turn to **1 Corinthians 12:28–30**. This passage contains a composite of gifts from all three groups. The ministry gifts mentioned here are apostles, prophets and teachers. The manifestation gifts mentioned are miracles, healings, tongues and interpretation of tongues. The motive gifts mentioned are serving (helping others) and administration.

2. This passage highlights the foundational truth that even though we may have different gifts, we are all important and necessary to the body of Christ.

EACH WEEK YOU WILL TEACH THE INTRODUCTION OF THE MOTIVE GIFTS THAT WILL BE ILLUSTRATED IN THE FOLLOWING WEEK'S SCRIPTURE ASSIGNMENT. FOR EXAMPLE, DURING THIS LESSON YOU WILL PRESENT THE INTRODUCTION OF THE *PERCEPTION* AND *SERVING* MOTIVE GIFTS THAT CLASS MEMBERS WILL PREPARE TO DISCUSS NEXT WEEK.

V. Introduction of the Perception and Serving Motive Gifts

A. Perception (Prophecy) Motive Gift

People with this gift have an acute intuitive sense about the true condition and position of people and situations in relation to God. They are able to discern the inner motives of people in a way others do not perceive. Their basic tendency is to view any person, group or situation in light of what God's Word says.

Each of the motive gifts can be related to a part of the human body, to help describe the function it serves.

1. Part of the body: The *eye*. Individuals with this motive gift receive spiritual insights.

2. Words describing people with this gift include persuasive, sensitive, honest, loyal and responsible.

3. The Greek word for *prophecy* is *propheteia* (prof-ay-ti´-ah), which comes from *prophetes* (prof-ay´-tace), meaning "an inspired speaker."[4]

4. *Vincent's Word Studies of the New Testament* describes this gift as follows: "In the New Testament, as in the Old, the prominent idea is not prediction, but the inspired delivery of warning, exhortation, instruction, judging, and making manifest the secrets of the heart."[5]

5. People who operate mainly in the perception motive gift are especially sensitive to perceiving the will of God. Then, depending upon the Lord's direction, they then proclaim it or pray for it to be accomplished.

Lesson 3 — Motive Gifts

All of us can give counsel and pray, but how we give counsel and pray will differ according to our motive gift.

6. In counsel and prayer:

    a. Perceivers are very Scripture-based. It is wonderful to see them turn to God's Word and use it in powerful ways to set people free.

    b. They see sin clearly and must be careful to avoid being judgmental as they give counsel and pray for others.

7. In ministry:

    All people can teach, but when perceivers teach, they will see things as either black or white, with no gray areas. They teach from Scripture. Their words often bring repentance. They prefer teaching older youths and adults.

    Each person with a motive gift can minister by leading a Bible study, but the subject, approach and desire will differ with each gift.

8. In leading a Bible study:

    a. Perceivers spend much time in prayerful preparation.

    b. They use the Bible as the basic text.

    c. They focus on subjects like prayer, prophecy and God's will.

d. They can't tolerate sin in people's lives. They want to see complete repentance and change in response to their teaching.

9. Related Scripture:

   "I know your deeds, that you are neither cold nor hot. I wish you were either one or the other! So, because you are lukewarm—neither hot nor cold—I will spit you out of my mouth" Revelation 3:15–16.

B. Serving Motive Gift

1. Part of the body: The *hands*. Individuals with this motive gift help complete projects.
2. Words that describe people with this gift include helpful, reliable, sensitive, obedient and hard working.
3. The Greek word for *serving* is *diakonia* (dee-ak-on-ee´-ah), which conveys the idea of doing practical things in order to be of service to others. Servers receive joy from helping, carrying out instructions, and being of use in a wide variety of ways.[6]
4. *Vincent's Word Studies of the New Testament* defines *serving* as "an activity of a practical nature exerted in action, not word."[7]
5. Servers are gifted with their hands and are equipped with physical stamina with disregard for weariness. They notice and understand what needs to be done. Unlike people with prophecy motive gifts who are often misunderstood because of the things that

they say, servers are often misunderstood because of the things they do.

All of us can give counsel and pray, but how we give counsel and pray will differ according to our motive gift.

6. In counsel and prayer:

    a. People with a serving motive gift help us to see areas of needed service or incidences of ungratefulness that we have overlooked.

    b. They will pray for the needs of others—wanting practical things to be accomplished in the life of the person for whom they are praying.

    c. They want so desperately to see God meet a person's needs that they may unconsciously interfere and hinder what God is trying to teach and do in that person's life.

7. In ministry:

    a. Servers make good Sunday school teachers, especially in the lower grades.

    b. Deacons often have serving as their motive gift.

    c. Servers often have the gift of hospitality.

    d. They enjoy assisting others, e.g., helping in the nursery or doing custodial or secretarial work.

Each person with a motive gift can minister by leading a Bible study, but the subject, approach and desire will differ with each gift.

8. In leading a Bible study:

    a. Servers usually prefer to use prepared materials.

    b. They do a detailed preparation of the lesson.

    c. Servers often focus on practical subjects that demonstrate faith.

9. Related Scripture:

    "Serve wholeheartedly, as if you were serving the Lord, not men, because you know that the Lord will reward everyone for whatever good he does…" Ephesians 6:7–8.

VI. Perception and Serving Gift Questionnaires

ASK PARTICIPANTS TO TURN TO THE QUESTIONNAIRES IN THE MOTIVE GIFT BOOKLET FOR THE GIFT OF PERCEPTION (PROPHECY) AND THE GIFT OF SERVING. PARTICIPANTS SHOULD FILL OUT THESE QUESTIONNAIRES NOW.

A. Instructions

   1. REVIEW THE SCORING INSTRUCTIONS ON PAGE 2.

Lesson 3 — Motive Gifts

2. As the first paragraph on page 3 says, "Don't answer the way you'd *like* to be or the way you think you *ought* to be. Be honest!" Be resolute in scoring. Don't be afraid to give yourself a zero or five, if they apply. Avoid being non-committal, giving yourself a two or three, unless those scores are really accurate!

3. Pay attention to the "typical problem areas." These might help you better understand some of the corresponding "characteristics." Most people have one predominant gift, sometimes two. If your scores are similar in three or more gifts, most likely you have not been totally honest with yourself!

4. Remember, the purpose of this test is to reveal your gift—and to enjoy the freedom this can bring to your walk with God.

B. Participants' Questionnaire Results

1. *BRIEFLY* REVIEW AND DISCUSS THE CLASS MEMBERS' RESULTS.

2. ASK IF ANYONE SCORED HIGH IN ONE OF THESE GIFTS. NOTE WHICH PARTICIPANTS FELT PERCEPTION OR SERVING MAY BE THEIR MOTIVE GIFT.

3. It is important that you encourage each participant as he gets revelation regarding his motive gift. If you agree that he has identified his motive gift, you might mention a situation when you saw the participant display characteristics connected with that motive gift.

4. PERSONAL COMMENTS SHOULD BE ENCOURAGING, BUT NOT INVOLVE FLATTERY, AND SHOULD NOT FOCUS ON A PARTICIPANT'S FAULTS.

VII. Discussion of the Assigned Article

ENCOURAGE THE DISCUSSION LEADER AND PARTICIPANTS TO FOCUS ON PORTIONS OF THE ARTICLE ASSIGNMENT THAT ARE IMPORTANT FOR THIS CLASS TO DISCUSS, ESPECIALLY AS IT RELATES TO THE MAIN PRINCIPLE.

VIII. Next Week's Assignment

A. REVIEW WITH THE CLASS NEXT WEEK'S ASSIGNMENT ON THE COURSE OUTLINE.

B. REVIEW THE MAIN PRINCIPLE FOR NEXT WEEK'S CLASS.

C. ASSIGN ONE CLASS MEMBER TO LEAD THE BOOK DISCUSSION AND ANOTHER FOR THE ASSIGNED ARTICLE DISCUSSION FOR LESSON 4.

D. ASSIGN EACH MOTIVE GIFT SCRIPTURE DISCUSSION TO A PARTICIPANT WHO IS STRONG IN EITHER THE **PERCEPTION** OR **SERVING** MOTIVE GIFT. THEY SHOULD EACH ALLOT ONLY 10 MINUTES FOR THEIR MOTIVE GIFT DISCUSSION. IF NO PARTICIPANT SCORED HIGH IN A SPECIFIC MOTIVE GIFT, THE

Lesson 3 — Motive Gifts

FACILITATOR SHOULD LEAD THAT SCRIPTURE DISCUSSION.

NOTES TO THE FACILITATOR:
YOU NEED TO CALL OR VISIT THE LESSON 4 DISCUSSION LEADERS DURING THE WEEK BEFORE THAT CLASS. SEE THE **APPENDIX** FOR QUESTIONS YOU CAN USE DURING THESE CONVERSATIONS TO HELP THE LEADERS PREPARE FOR THIS CLASS. REMEMBER TO CALL THE DISCUSSION LEADERS DURING THE WEEK BEFORE *EACH* LESSON.

IX. Ministry Time

A. AS FACILITATOR, YOU NEED TO GUIDE THE MINISTRY TIME. REFER TO THE CLASS FORMAT SECTION OF THE *FACILITATOR TRAINING STUDY GUIDE* AND READ THE MINISTRY TIME SECTION. (Note: This *Facilitator Training Study Guide* is the book you received during Facilitator Training.)

B. DURING THE MINISTRY TIME, WE SUGGEST THAT YOU DO NOT ASK CLASS MEMBERS FOR THEIR PRAYER REQUESTS. SAY TO THE PARTICIPANTS, "In general, in this course we wait until Lesson 4 to begin personal prayer ministry. In Lesson 4 during the ministry time, we will begin praying for participants who have the motive gift discussed in that lesson."

C. ON THE OTHER HAND, IF YOU SENSE THE LORD DIRECTING YOU TO ADDRESS THE NEED FOR PERSONAL PRAYER MINISTRY

IN A CLASS MEMBER, ASK THE PERSON CONCERNED IF HE WOULD LIKE PRAYER.

D. INITIALLY, YOU MAY NEED TO DO THE MINISTERING, THEREBY SETTING THE EXAMPLE FOR THE CLASS.

E. AT THE BEGINNING OF THE MINISTRY TIME REMIND PARTICIPANTS ABOUT THE FOLLOWING:

As we minister to each other, we need to recognize that we are all fine-tuning our hearing of God's voice. We may not hear clearly all the time, so we need to carefully weigh any word of prophecy a class member gives us. The following is a helpful guideline:

If it doesn't make sense, put it on the shelf. If it contradicts what God has told you, let it drop. If your spirit confirms it, make a note of it in your journal and watch God bring it about.

F. ENCOURAGE HANDS-ON MINISTRY BY CLASS MEMBERS. ALLOW THE GIFTS OF THE SPIRIT TO MANIFEST IN DIFFERENT PEOPLE.

G. BE CAREFUL THAT ONE PERSON DOES NOT DOMINATE THE MINISTERING.

H. CLOSE THE CLASS WITH PRAYER. (SEE SAMPLE PRAYER IN LESSON 2).

IN CHRIST

LESSON 4

MOTIVE GIFTS–
PERCEPTION AND SERVING

MAIN PRINCIPLE

People with a perception motive gift perform the function of the eye for the body of Christ, while servers perform the function of the hands.

LESSON 4

Motive Gifts– Perception and Serving

I. Let's Get Started!

    A. WELCOME THE CLASS.

    B. OPEN WITH PRAYER.

    C. WORSHIP THE LORD.

    D. READ, OR HAVE SOMEONE READ, THE MAIN PRINCIPLE FOR TODAY'S LESSON.

II. Supporting Principles From the Book

ENCOURAGE THE DISCUSSION LEADER AND PARTICIPANTS TO FOCUS ON PORTIONS OF THE BOOK ASSIGNMENT THAT ARE IMPORTANT FOR THIS CLASS TO DISCUSS, ESPECIALLY AS IT RELATES TO THE MAIN PRINCIPLE.

III. Supporting Principles From Scripture—
Luke 3:2–20
Luke 10:38–42
John 12:2

FACILITATORS: PRIOR TO THIS LESSON BE SURE THAT YOU HAVE REVIEWED THE FOLLOWING LISTED VERSES AND CHARACTERISTICS. THIS WILL HELP YOU ADD TO THE DISCUSSION, IF NEEDED.

Lesson 4 — Motive Gifts—Perception and Serving

ALLOW ONLY 10 MINUTES FOR EACH MOTIVE GIFT SCRIPTURE DISCUSSION. IF A HIGH-SCORING PARTICIPANT IS LEADING A DISCUSSION, REMIND HIM OF THAT TIME CONSTRAINT.

A. **The Biblical Motive Gift of Perception[1]— Luke 3:2–20**

As we read **Luke 3:2–20**, we can conclude that John the Baptist had the motive gift of perception (prophecy). Turn to your test entitled **"The Gift of Perception."**

1. John the Baptist is preaching all around the Jordan River. What is he preaching? (See **verses 3, 7**.)

2. Looking at **verse 3**, what characteristics of the gift of perception can you identify in John? (1, 3, 4, 9, 11, 20)

3. Do you think John exemplifies characteristic #18— Has strong opinions and convictions? Why?

4. Are there any other characteristics you see in John that stem from the perception motive gift?

   verse 2—Characteristics 13, 15
   verse 7—12, 16, 18
   verse 8—4, 8, 10, 12, 16, 18
   verse 9—8, 10, 16, 18
   verse 10—10
   verse 11—2, 8, 14
   verse 12—2, 10, 14, 18
   verse 16—13, 14, 20
   verse 17—2, 13, 20
   verse 18—10, 13, 20

verse 19—2, 18
verse 20—20

5. Can you see in John any of the typical problems associated with the perception motive gift?

6. If you had this motive gift, and you recognized in yourself some of the associated problem areas, what steps could you take to minimize these problem areas?

B. **The Biblical Motive Gift of Serving**[2]—
Luke 10:38–42
John 12:2

As we read **Luke 10:38–42** and **John 12:2** we might conclude that Martha had the motive gift of serving. Refer to your test entitled **"The Gift of Serving."**

1. In **Luke 10:38** we can see that Martha showed love for others through her actions. What other characteristics do you see in Martha in **Luke 10:38–42** that show she was operating out of a serving motive gift? (1, 5, 12)

2. What do you think Martha's house was like? Do you think she kept it very neat? (16, 17)

3. Can you see in Martha any serving characteristics that could have led to this display of irritation with Mary?
verse 40—4, 12, 17, 18
verse 41—4, 12, 17
verse 42—18

Lesson 4 — Motive Gifts—Perception and Serving

4. Can you see in Martha any of the typical problems associated with the serving motive gift?
   verse 40—Problem #1
   verse 41—Problem #5
   verse 42—Problem #2

5. What serving characteristics do you see in Martha in **John 12:2**? (5, 10, 20)

6. If you sense that you have this motive gift, and you recognize in yourself some of the associated problem areas, what steps could you take to minimize these problem areas?

TEACH THE FOLLOWING SECTION. IT IS AN INTRODUCTION TO THE MOTIVE GIFTS WHICH THE CLASS WILL DISCUSS NEXT WEEK.

IV. Introduction to the Motive Gifts of Teaching and Exhortation

A. Teaching

Teachers tend to believe that their gift is foundational to the other gifts. Teachers love to read and study, and place great emphasis on the accuracy of facts and words. They may receive more joy from doing research than from presenting the material.

Each of the motive gifts can be related to a part of the human body, to help describe the function it serves.

1. Part of the body: The *head*—Teachers want to increase people's understanding.[3]

2. Words that describe individuals with this gift include comprehending, diligent, perfectionist and dependable.

3. The Greek word for *teaching* is *didasko* (did-as´-ko), which means to teach or give instruction.[4] People with the teaching motive gift are often drawn into areas of research. They may do teaching through writing papers, articles, dissertations or books rather than teaching in person.

All of us can give counsel and pray, but how we give counsel and pray will differ according to our motive gift.

4. Because people with the teaching motive gift want to clarify truth, you'll see them giving counsel and praying, using scriptural instruction and explanation.

5. In ministry:

    a. Not all people with this gift are called into full-time ministry as teachers.

    b. They generally prefer teaching adult or college-age classes, or preparing and providing enrichment materials.

Each person with a motive gift can minister by leading a Bible study, but the subject, approach and desire will differ with each gift.

6. In leading a Bible study:

    a. Teachers want to prepare their own lesson plans.

b. They spend significant amounts of time in biblical research.

   c. Teachers generally prefer teaching an entire book of the Bible (as opposed to an incomplete portion) or a specific topic.

7. Related Scriptures:
   "For the word of God is living and active. Sharper than any double-edged sword, it penetrates even to dividing soul and spirit, joints and marrow; it judges the thoughts and attitudes of the heart" Hebrews 4:12.

   "…So is my word that goes out from my mouth: It will not return to me empty, but will accomplish what I desire and achieve the purpose for which I sent it" Isaiah 55:11.

B. Exhortation

Exhortation is a gift, which centers on life experience. Unlike the teacher, truth is truth for the exhorter—whether it comes from the Bible or from experience. In fact, the exhorter needs to confirm the truth of Scripture by experience. When exhorters speak, they greatly desire the full interest and attention of every listener, for the focus of their gift is the individual and his or her personal growth.

   1. Part of the body: The *mouth*—People with this motive gift communicate words of love.

   2. Words that describe exhorters include loving, obedient and happy.

3. The Greek word for *exhortation* is *paraklesis* (par-ak´-lay-sis), which denotes the making of an earnest appeal, entreaty, consolation and comfort.[5]

4. While teachers aim for the mind, exhorters aim for the heart and the will.[6] It is not so much the content that exhorters want to impart, as how that content can be made effective in people's lives.

All of us can give counsel and pray, but how we give counsel and pray will differ according to our motive gift.

5. In counsel and prayer:

    a. Exhorters pray, using prayers of encouragement.

    b. In giving counsel they will refer to personal experience, if possible. They like saying, "I've had the same thing happen to me."

    c. Exhorters make excellent counselors. They can pinpoint problems and give helpful step-by-step solutions.

6. In ministry:

    a. All the motive gifts can teach, but exhorters make learning the most interesting and applicable.

    b. Exhorters are happy teaching any age group, but will be especially adept with children and teenagers.

Each person with a motive gift can minister by leading a Bible study, but the subject, approach and desire will differ with each gift.

Lesson 4 — Motive Gifts—Perception and Serving

7. In leading a Bible study:

   a. Exhorters prefer using prepared materials.

   b. They draw from life experiences for illustrations.

   c. They most often choose subjects that help people live victoriously.

8. Related Scripture:
   "Let us not give up meeting together, as some are in the habit of doing, but let us encourage one another—and all the more as you see the Day approaching" Hebrews 10:25.

V. Teaching and Exhortation Gift Questionnaires

ASK PARTICIPANTS TO TURN TO THE QUESTIONNAIRES IN THE MOTIVE GIFT BOOKLET FOR THE GIFT OF TEACHING AND THE GIFT OF EXHORTATION. PARTICIPANTS SHOULD FILL OUT THESE QUESTIONNAIRES NOW.

A. Instructions

1. ASK IF ANYONE HAS ANY QUESTIONS ABOUT HOW TO FILL OUT THE QUESTIONNAIRES. REVIEW THE INSTRUCTIONS, IF NEEDED.

2. Remember: Don't answer as you'd *prefer* to be or the way you think you *ought* to be. Be honest! Be resolute in scoring. Don't be afraid to give yourself a zero or five, if they apply. Avoid taking the easy

route by giving yourself a two or three, unless they are really true!

3. Pay attention to the "typical problem areas." These might help you better understand some of the corresponding characteristics. Most people have one predominant gift, sometimes two. If you get a similar score in three or more gifts, most likely you have not been honest with yourself!

4. Remember: The purpose of this test is to reveal your gift—and to enjoy the freedom this can bring to your walk with God.

B. Participants' Questionnaire Results

1. *BRIEFLY* REVIEW AND DISCUSS THE CLASS MEMBERS' RESULTS.

2. ASK IF ANYONE SCORED HIGH IN ONE OF THESE GIFTS.

3. IT IS IMPORTANT THAT YOU ENCOURAGE EACH PARTICPANT AS THEY GET REVELATION REGARDING THEIR MOTIVE GIFT. IF YOU AGREE THAT THEY HAVE IDENTIFIED THEIR MOTIVE GIFT, YOU MIGHT MENTION A SITUATION WHEN YOU SAW THE PARTICIPANT DISPLAY CHARACTERISTICS CONNECTED WITH THAT MOTIVE GIFT.

4. PERSONAL COMMENTS SHOULD BE ENCOURAGING, BUT NOT INVOLVE FLATTERY, AND SHOULD NOT FOCUS ON A PARTICIPANT'S FAULTS.

VI. Discussion of the Assigned Article

ENCOURAGE THE DISCUSSION LEADER AND PARTICIPANTS TO FOCUS ON PORTIONS OF THE ARTICLE ASSIGNMENT THAT ARE IMPORTANT FOR THIS CLASS TO DISCUSS, ESPECIALLY AS IT RELATES TO THE MAIN PRINCIPLE.

VII. Next Week's Assignment

A. REVIEW WITH THE CLASS NEXT WEEK'S ASSIGNMENT ON THE COURSE OUTLINE.

B. REVIEW THE MAIN PRINCIPLE FOR NEXT WEEK'S CLASS.

C. ASSIGN ONE OR TWO CLASS MEMBERS TO LEAD THE BOOK DISCUSSION FOR LESSON 5.

D. ASSIGN EACH MOTIVE GIFT SCRIPTURE DISCUSSION TO A PARTICIPANT WHO IS STRONG IN EITHER THE **TEACHING** OR **EXHORTATION** MOTIVE GIFT. THEY SHOULD EACH ALLOT ONLY 10 MINUTES FOR THEIR MOTIVE GIFT DISCUSSION. IF NO PARTICPANT SCORED HIGH IN A SPECIFIC MOTIVE GIFT, THE FACILITATOR SHOULD LEAD THAT SCRIPTURE DISCUSSION.

NOTES TO THE FACILITATOR:
YOU NEED TO CALL OR VISIT THE LESSON 5 DISCUSSION LEADERS DURING THE WEEK BEFORE THAT CLASS. SEE THE **APPENDIX** FOR

QUESTIONS YOU CAN USE DURING THESE CONVERSATIONS TO HELP THE LEADERS PREPARE FOR THIS CLASS. REMEMBER TO CALL THE DISCUSSION LEADERS DURING THE WEEK BEFORE *EACH* LESSON.

VIII. Ministry Time

A. AS FACILITATOR, YOU NEED TO GUIDE THE MINISTRY TIME. REFER TO THE CLASS FORMAT SECTION OF THE *FACILITATOR TRAINING STUDY GUIDE* AND READ THE MINISTRY TIME SECTION. (Note: The *Facilitator Training Study Guide* is the book you received during Facilitator Training.)

B. YOU HAVE THE OPTION OF WAITING UNTIL LESSON 7 TO MINISTER TO **ALL** PARTICIPANTS RELATED TO THEIR MOTIVE GIFTS, AFTER ALL THE MOTIVE GIFTS HAVE BEEN DISCUSSED. OTHERWISE, BE SURE TO PRAY FOR PARTICIPANTS WHO THINK THEY HAVE THE **PERCEPTION** OR **SERVING** MOTIVE GIFT TODAY. BELOW FIND SOME RELEVANT SCRIPTURES. AS YOU PREPARE TO MINISTER TO THESE PARTICIPANTS, ASK THE HOLY SPIRIT WHETHER YOU SHOULD PRAY FROM THESE VERSES, OR OTHERS, IN THE MINISTRY TIME, OR PERHAPS GIVE THEM TO INDIVIDUALS AT AN APPROPRIATE TIME.

For the Perception motive gift:
"**He who loves purity *and* the pure in heart *and* who is gracious in speech—because of the grace of his lips will he have the king for his friend**" Proverbs **22:11 (AMP)**.

Lesson 4 — Motive Gifts—Perception and Serving

"...Be an example to all believers in what you say, in the way you live, in your love, your faith, and your purity" 1 Timothy 4:12 b (NLT).

For the Serving motive gift:
"Serve the Lord with reverent fear, and rejoice with trembling" Psalm 2:11 (NLT).

"Do you have the gift of helping others? Do it with all the strength and energy that God supplies. Then everything you do will bring glory to God through Jesus Christ. All glory and power to him forever and ever! Amen" 1 Peter 4:11b (NLT).

C. ALSO, INCLUDE THE FOLLOWING IN THIS MINISTRY TIME:

Thank You, Lord, for placing this motive gift in *this person*. Show *him* how to use this gift according to Your will. Help *him* grow in maturity and understanding so that *he* can bring unity to the Body of Christ and be transformed more into the likeness of Christ.

D. NOTE: UNLESS YOU HAVE DECIDED TO WAIT UNTIL LESSON 7, THE MINISTRY EMPHASIS HAS NOW SHIFTED TO PARTICIPANTS WITH SPECIFIC MOTIVE GIFTS. ANY OTHER PERSONAL MINISTRY SHOULD NOW BE GIVEN A LOWER PRIORITY AND MAY NEED TO BE ADDRESSED AFTER CLASS.

E. INITIALLY, YOU MAY NEED TO DO THE MINISTERING, THEREBY SETTING THE EXAMPLE FOR THE CLASS.

F. AT THE BEGINNING OF THE MINISTRY TIME, REMIND PARTICIPANTS ABOUT THE FOLLOWING:

As we minister to each other, we need to recognize that we are all fine-tuning our hearing of God's voice. We may not hear clearly all the time, so we need to carefully weigh any word of prophecy a class member gives us. The following is a helpful guideline:

If it doesn't make sense, put it on the shelf. If it contradicts what God has told you, let it drop. If your spirit confirms it, make a note of it in your journal and watch God bring it about.

G. ENCOURAGE HANDS-ON MINISTRY BY CLASS MEMBERS. ALLOW THE GIFTS OF THE SPIRIT TO MANIFEST IN DIFFERENT PEOPLE.

H. CLOSE THE CLASS WITH PRAYER. (SEE SAMPLE PRAYER IN LESSON 2).

IN CHRIST

LESSON 5

MOTIVE GIFTS— TEACHING AND EXHORTATION

MAIN PRINCIPLE

People with the teaching motive gift perform the function of the mind for the body of Christ, while exhorters act as the mouth.

WWW.ZOEMINISTRIES.ORG

LESSON 5

Motive Gifts— Teaching and Exhortation

I. Let's Get Started!

   A. WELCOME THE CLASS.

   B. OPEN WITH PRAYER.

   C. WORSHIP THE LORD.

   D. READ, OR HAVE SOMEONE READ, THE MAIN PRINCIPLE FOR TODAY'S LESSON.

II. Supporting Principles From the Book

ENCOURAGE THE DISCUSSION LEADER AND PARTICIPANTS TO FOCUS ON PORTIONS OF THE BOOK ASSIGNMENT THAT ARE IMPORTANT FOR THIS CLASS TO DISCUSS, ESPECIALLY AS IT RELATES TO THE MAIN PRINCIPLE.

III. Review of Last Week's Motive Gifts

   A. **Perception**—A person with this gift acts as the eye of the body of Christ by seeing where people and situations are in light of God's Word. He can deliver an inspired warning, exhortation, instruction, or judgment, and can make manifest the secrets of the heart.[1]

B. **Serving**—A person with this gift acts as the hands of the body of Christ by doing practical things and being of service to others. He seems to "see" what needs to be done and use his great stamina to help in a variety of ways.

IV. Supporting Principles From Scripture—
Acts 18:24–28
1 Corinthians 3:6
Acts 4:36; 11:22–26
Acts 14:1–26
Acts 15:2–3, 35–41

FACILITATORS: PRIOR TO THIS LESSON BE SURE THAT YOU HAVE REVIEWED THE FOLLOWING LISTED VERSES AND CHARACTERISTICS. THIS WILL HELP YOU ADD TO THE DISCUSSION, IF NEEDED.

ALLOW ONLY 10 MINUTES FOR EACH MOTIVE GIFT SCRIPTURE DISCUSSION. IF A HIGH-SCORING PARTICIPANT IS LEADING A DISCUSSION, REMIND HIM OF THAT TIME CONSTRAINT.

A. **The Biblical Motive Gift of Teaching**[2]—
Acts 18:24–28
1 Corinthians 3:6

As we read the assigned Scriptures we can see that Apollos had the motive gift of teaching. Turn to your test entitled **"The Gift of Teaching."**

1. In **Acts 18:24–28** Apollos was teaching the Scriptures thoroughly and with boldness. Which

of the teaching motive characteristics do you see in Apollos?
verse 24—Characteristics #1, 3, 9, 15
verse 25—1, 2, 3, 5, 13, 16
verse 26—7, 19
verse 27—12, 15, 19
verse 28—1, 9, 13, 15, 19

2. Which teaching motive characteristics do you see in Apollos in **1 Corinthians 3:6**? (12, 20)

3. After they heard Apollos, Priscilla and Aquila took him aside and explained the way of God more accurately. One of the problem areas of a teaching motive is being slow to accept the viewpoints of others. How do you think Apollos might have reacted?

4. If you have this motive gift, and you recognize in yourself some of the associated problem areas, what steps could you take to minimize these problem areas?

B. The Biblical Motive Gift of Exhortation[3]—
Acts 4:36; 11:22–26
Acts 14:1–26
Acts 15:2–3, 35–41

As we read the assigned Scriptures we can conclude that Barnabas had the motive gift of exhortation. Refer to your test entitled **"The Gift of Exhortation."**

1. In **Acts 4:36** we read that Barnabas was originally Joseph, a Levite of Cyprian birth. He then was called Barnabas, which means son of encouragement. He obviously exhibited

Lesson 5 — Motive Gifts—Teaching and Exhortation

characteristic #1. What other characteristics may be seen in this verse? (#14)

2. Turn in your Bible to **Acts 11:22–26**.

   a. We see Barnabas was sent to the church in Antioch. Do you think that Barnabas had characteristic #11—being fluent in communication? Why?

   b. What are the characteristics you see in Barnabas in **verse 23**? (1, 7, 9, 13, 14, 19) Do you see any of these characteristics in yourself or in anyone in the class?

   c. In **verse 25**, why do you think he went looking for Saul? Was it because he needed a "sounding board" for bouncing off ideas as is mentioned in #20? What other characteristics possibly motivated Barnabas to find Saul? (1, 6, 7, 11, 13)

   d. In **verse 26**, what characteristics might explain why Barnabas stayed in Antioch for an entire year? (1, 3, 4, 6, 9, 17)

   e. Do you see any other exhortation characteristics in Barnabas in **Acts 11:22–26**? (2, 15)

3. Turn to **Acts 14:1–26**.

   a. What characteristics do you see in Barnabas in **verses 1–3**? (4, 6, 11)

   b. What characteristics do you see in Barnabas in **verses 15–26**?
   verse 15—13, 18
   verse 17—8

How To Hear God's Voice—In Christ

      verse 20—1, 12
      verse 21—6, 11
      verse 22—1, 5, 6, 12, 15, 19
      verse 23—7
      verse 26—17

4. Turn to **Acts 15:2–3, 35–41**.

   a. In **verses 2–3**, what characteristics in Barnabas and Paul influenced the Antioch believers to send them to Jerusalem? (11, 14, 18)

   b. In **verses 35–41**, what characteristics in Barnabas might cause him to disagree with Paul? (1, 6, 7, 9, 13, 14, 17)

   c. What do you think of Paul and Barnabas separating and going their own ways? Which of the typical problem areas do you see as possibly contributing to Barnabas' decision? (1, 3, 4)

5. If you have this motive gift, and you recognize in yourself some of the associated problem areas, what steps could you take to minimize these problem areas?

V. Introduction to the Motive Gifts of Giving and Administration

A. Giving Motive Gift

The real motivation behind those who have the gift of giving is to support others by sharing what they have. They are not gullible—they have insight about when and whom to help. This gift is not restricted to the wealthy;

money is only one concrete expression of this gift. Givers have well-rounded personalities, having many of the traits of the other motive gifts. They can be leaders or followers. Givers, like servers, want to give practical help. Like those with the gifts of prophecy and teaching, they have a love for the Word.[4]

Each of the motive gifts can be related to a part of the human body, to help describe the function it serves.

1. Part of the body: *Arms* extended—One always feels their strong support as they give what they have.

2. Words that describe individuals with this gift include generous, helpful, kind, honest and thrifty.

3. The Greek word for *giving* is *metadidomi* (met-ad-id´-o-mee), which means to give over, share or impart.[5] This action is to be done with *haplotes* (hap-lot´-ace)—simplicity, sincerity and liberality.[6]

4. Givers share and give from their earthly possessions.[7] Of all the motive gifts, this gift is the least likely to be recognized by the ones who have it.

All of us can give counsel and pray, but how we give counsel and pray will differ according to our motive gift.

5. In counsel and prayer:

    a. Givers can help reveal unwise use of assets.

    b. It is important to pull these people into counsel for their God-given expertise on fund-raising and distribution of funds.

c. The body of Christ is blessed by their wisdom.

6. In ministry:

    a. Givers typically serve well on advisory boards, as elders, or as financial advisers.

    b. They can be adept at teaching any age group. They do well at teaching about giving.

    c. Givers often want to handle finances or promote missionary support.

Each person with a motive gift can minister by leading a Bible study, but the subject, approach and desire will differ with each gift.

7. In leading a Bible study:

    a. Givers usually enjoy doing their own preparations.

    b. They may gear their lesson toward winning someone to Christ.

    c. They may focus on subjects like evangelism and missions.

8. Related Scripture:
   "The Lord Jesus himself said, 'It is more blessed to give than receive' " Acts 20:35.

B. Administration Motive Gift

Administrators provide leadership by working with and through others. Unlike servers, leaders do not take joy in doing the task themselves. They "maintain" the church by making things easier for others. They help the Body define and accomplish goals and tasks by providing leadership support.

1. Part of the body: The *shoulders*—They are willing to carry responsibility.

2. Words that describe individuals with the gift of administration include diligent, capable, responsible, honest and gregarious. Titles that have been used to describe people with this motive gift are facilitator, organizer, ruler, leader or superintendent.

3. The Greek word for *administration* is *proistemi* (pro-is´-tay-mee), which means "to stand before" and "to preside."[8]

4. *The Word Studies New Testament* indicates that the term *administrator* refers to any position involving superintendence.[9]

All of us can give counsel and pray, but how we give counsel and pray will differ according to our motive gift.

5. In counsel and prayer:

    a. Administrators tend to be discerning, and know who and what will work to help an individual reach his or her potential.

    b. They can help by pointing out mismanagement of time or by recommending procedures that will best accomplish goals.

    c. Administrators like to stand back and see the body of Christ operating smoothly.

d. They often know who needs to come forth with prayer in ministry.

   e. When praying, they seem to know how to "stand in the gap" for a specific need.

6. In ministry:

   a. Administrators love a challenge. They love to "dig in" and develop or organize anything within their area of influence.

   b. Their natural motivation is a creative desire to take raw materials—and even people—to help bring something new into existence.

   c. Administrators, by job requirement, need to be "jacks of all trades, but masters of none." In order to supervise effectively, they need to know a little about everything. They will have a wide range of interests and abilities, but the people with whom they work will be more capable and specialized in performing specific tasks.

Each person with a motive gift can minister by leading a Bible study, but the subject, approach and desire will differ with each gift.

7. In leading a Bible study:

   a. Administrators will probably organize materials into their own special lesson plans.

   b. They may bring in resource people for added interest.

Lesson 5 — Motive Gifts—Teaching and Exhortation

    c. They tend to cover broad subjects from a variety of different aspects.

    d. They will focus on teaching for discipleship and training one-on-one.

8. Related Scripture:
    "All things should be done with regard to decency *and* propriety and in an orderly fashion" 1 Corinthians 14:40 (AMP).

VI. Giving and Administration Gift Questionnaires

ASK PARTICIPANTS TO TURN TO THE QUESTIONNAIRES IN THE MOTIVE GIFT BOOKLET FOR THE GIFT OF GIVING AND THE GIFT OF ADMINISTRATION. PARTICIPANTS SHOULD FILL OUT THESE QUESTIONNAIRES NOW.

A. Instructions
   REPEAT THE FOLLOWING REMINDERS, IF NECESSARY:

   1. Remember: Don't answer as you'd *prefer* to be or the way you think you *ought* to be. Be honest! Be resolute in scoring. Don't be afraid to give yourself a zero or five, if they apply. Avoid taking the easy route by giving yourself a two or three, unless they are really true!

   2. Pay attention to the "typical problem areas." These might help you better understand some of the corresponding characteristics. Most people have *one* predominant gift, sometimes two. If you get a

similar score in three or more gifts, most likely you have not been honest with yourself!

3. Remember: The purpose of this test is to reveal your gifting—and to enjoy the freedom this can bring to your walk with God.

B. Participants' Questionnaire Results

1. *BRIEFLY* REVIEW AND DISCUSS THE CLASS MEMBERS' RESULTS.

2. ASK IF ANYONE SCORED HIGH IN ONE OF THESE GIFTS.

3. IT IS IMPORTANT THAT YOU ENCOURAGE EACH PARTICIPANT AS HE GETS REVELATION REGARDING HIS MOTIVE GIFT. IF YOU AGREE THAT HE HAS IDENTIFIED HIS MOTIVE GIFT, YOU MIGHT MENTION A SITUATION WHEN YOU SAW THE PARTICIPANT DISPLAY CHARACTERISTICS CONNECTED WITH THAT MOTIVE GIFT.

4. PERSONAL COMMENTS SHOULD BE ENCOURAGING, BUT NOT INVOLVE FLATTERY, AND SHOULD NOT FOCUS ON A PARTICIPANT'S FAULTS.

VII. Next Week's Assignment

A. REVIEW WITH THE CLASS NEXT WEEK'S ASSIGNMENT ON THE COURSE OUTLINE.

Lesson 5 — Motive Gifts—Teaching and Exhortation

    B. REVIEW THE MAIN PRINCIPLE FOR NEXT WEEK'S CLASS.

    C. ASSIGN ONE PARTICIPANT TO LEAD THE BOOK DISCUSSION AND ANOTHER FOR THE ASSIGNED ARTICLE DISCUSSION FOR LESSON 6.

    D. ASSIGN EACH MOTIVE GIFT SCRIPTURE DISCUSSION TO A PARTICIPANT WHO IS STRONG IN EITHER THE **GIVING** OR **ADMINISTRATION** MOTIVE GIFT. THEY SHOULD EACH ALLOT ONLY 10 MINUTES FOR THEIR MOTIVE GIFT DISCUSSION. IF NO PARTICPANT SCORED HIGH IN A SPECIFIC MOTIVE GIFT, THE FACILITATOR SHOULD LEAD THAT SCRIPTURE DISCUSSION.

NOTES TO THE FACILITATOR:
YOU NEED TO CALL OR VISIT THE LESSON 6 DISCUSSION LEADERS DURING THE WEEK BEFORE THAT CLASS. SEE THE **APPENDIX** FOR QUESTIONS YOU CAN USE DURING THESE CONVERSATIONS TO HELP THE LEADERS PREPARE FOR THIS CLASS. REMEMBER TO CALL THE DISCUSSION LEADERS DURING THE WEEK BEFORE *EACH* LESSON.

VIII. Ministry Time

    A. AS FACILITATOR, YOU NEED TO GUIDE THE MINISTRY TIME.

    B. BE SURE TO PRAY FOR PARTICIPANTS WHO THINK THEY HAVE THE **TEACHING** OR

EXHORTATION MOTIVE GIFT. BELOW FIND SOME RELEVANT SCRIPTURES. AS YOU PREPARE TO MINISTER TO THESE PARTICIPANTS, ASK THE HOLY SPIRIT WHETHER YOU SHOULD PRAY FROM THESE VERSES, OR OTHERS, IN THE MINISTRY TIME, OR PERHAPS GIVE THEM TO INDIVIDUALS AT AN APPROPRIATE TIME.

For the Teaching motive gift:
"**Do you have the gift of speaking? Then speak as though God himself were speaking through you**" 1 Peter 4:11a **(NLT)**.

"**And you yourself must be an example to them by doing good works of every kind. Let everything you do reflect the integrity and seriousness of your teaching**" Titus 2:7 **(NLT)**.

For the Exhortation motive gift:
"**I have sent him to you for this very purpose—to let you know how we are doing and to encourage you**" Colossians 4:8 **(NLT)**.

"**So encourage each other with these words**" 1 Thessalonians 4:18 **(NLT)**.

C. ALSO, INCLUDE THE FOLLOWING IN THIS MINISTRY TIME:

Thank You, Lord, for placing this motive gift in *this person*. Show *him* how to use this gift according to Your will. Help *him* grow in maturity and understanding so that *he* can bring unity to the Body of Christ and be transformed more into the likeness of Christ.

Lesson 5 — Motive Gifts—Teaching and Exhortation

D. NOTE: UNLESS YOU HAVE DECIDED TO WAIT UNTIL LESSON 7, THE MINISTRY EMPHASIS HAS NOW SHIFTED TO PARTICIPANTS WITH SPECIFIC MOTIVE GIFTS. ANY OTHER PERSONAL MINISTRY SHOULD NOW BE GIVEN A LOWER PRIORITY AND MAY NEED TO BE ADDRESSED AFTER CLASS.

E. INITIALLY, YOU MAY NEED TO DO THE MINISTERING, THEREBY SETTING THE EXAMPLE FOR THE CLASS.

F. AT THE BEGINNING OF THE MINISTRY TIME, REMIND PARTICIPANTS ABOUT THE FOLLOWING:

As we minister to each other, we need to recognize that we are all fine-tuning our hearing of God's voice. We may not hear clearly all the time, so we need to carefully weigh any word of prophecy a class member gives us. The following is a helpful guideline:

If it doesn't make sense, put it on the shelf. If it contradicts what God has told you, let it drop. If your spirit confirms it, make a note of it in your journal and watch God bring it about.

G. ENCOURAGE HANDS-ON MINISTRY BY CLASS MEMBERS. ALLOW THE GIFTS OF THE SPIRIT TO MANIFEST IN DIFFERENT PEOPLE.

H. CLOSE WITH PRAYER.

IN CHRIST

LESSON 6

MOTIVE GIFTS—
GIVING AND ADMINISTRATION

MAIN PRINCIPLE

People with a giving motive gift perform the function of extended arms, while people with the gift of administration serve as the shoulders of the body of Christ.

WWW.ZOEMINISTRIES.ORG

LESSON 6

Motive Gifts— Giving and Administration

I. Let's Get Started!

A. WELCOME THE CLASS.

B. OPEN WITH PRAYER.

C. WORSHIP THE LORD.

D. READ, OR HAVE SOMEONE READ, THE MAIN PRINCIPLE FOR TODAY'S LESSON.

II. Supporting Principles From the Book

ENCOURAGE THE DISCUSSION LEADER AND PARTICIPANTS TO FOCUS ON PORTIONS OF THE BOOK ASSIGNMENT THAT ARE IMPORTANT FOR THIS CLASS TO DISCUSS, ESPECIALLY AS IT RELATES TO THE MAIN PRINCIPLE.

III. Review of Last Week's Motive Gifts

A. **Teaching**—People with this gift act as the *head* of the body of Christ by clarifying truth and increasing people's understanding of God's Word.

B. **Exhortation**—People with this gift act as the *mouth* of the body of Christ by speaking words of encouragement or motivation. Their words are meant to strengthen the hearts and wills of believers so that we can live victoriously.

IV. Supporting Principles From Scripture—Genesis 13, 14, 37, 39, 41

FACILITATORS: PRIOR TO THIS LESSON BE SURE THAT YOU HAVE REVIEWED THE FOLLOWING LISTED VERSES AND CHARACTERISTICS. THIS WILL HELP YOU ADD TO THE DISCUSSION, IF NEEDED.

ALLOW ONLY 10 MINUTES FOR EACH MOTIVE GIFT SCRIPTURE DISCUSSION. IF A HIGH-SCORING PARTICIPANT IS LEADING A DISCUSSION, REMIND HIM OF THAT TIME CONSTRAINT.

A. The Biblical Motive Gift of Giving[1]**—Genesis 13 and 14**

As we read the assigned Scriptures, we can conclude that Abraham had the motive gift of giving. Turn to your test entitled **"The Gift of Giving."**

1. Turn to **Genesis 13:1–18**.

   a. In what verses do you see Abraham exhibiting characteristic #1—Gives freely of money, possessions, time, energy and love? (**verses 2 and 9**)

   b. What giving characteristics might explain Abraham's generosity in **verses 8–9**? (7, 15, 20)

c. What other giving characteristics do you see in this passage?
   verse 2—16
   verse 4—4
   verse 8—11
   verse 9—8
   verse 18—15

2. Turn to **Genesis 14:11–24**.

   a. When Abraham heard that his relative Lot had been taken captive, what did he do? (**verses 14–16**)

   b. In addition to Lot, what else did he bring back? (**verse 16**)

   c. In **verse 20**, do you think he was led by the Holy Spirit (characteristic #7)? What other characteristics of giving do you see in this verse? (1, 8, 15, 16)

   d. In **verses 23–24**, why did Abraham make that decision? Did this show characteristic #20—possesses both natural and God-given wisdom?

   e. What other giving characteristics do you see in this passage?
      verse 14—1, 11
      verse 16—1, 11, 16
      verse 22—14
      verse 23—15, 19

   f. Was there anything else in this passage that spoke to you about giving?

Lesson 6 — Motive Gifts—Giving and Administration

3. In this passage Abraham didn't seem to exhibit any of the typical problem areas. Which of these problem areas might negatively impact a church or family?

4. If you have this motive gift, and you recognize in yourself some of the associated problem areas, what steps could you take to minimize these problem areas?

B. **The Biblical Motive Gift of Administration[2]—Genesis 37, 39, 41**

As we read the assigned Scriptures, we see that Joseph had the motive gift of administration. Turn to your test entitled **"The Gift of Administration."**

1. Turn to **Genesis 37:1–11**.

    a. Israel (formerly called Jacob) loved Joseph more than he loved his other sons because Joseph was the first born of his favorite wife, Rachel, and he was the son of his old age (**Genesis 29:20; 30:22–24**.)

    Knowing that Joseph was favored by his father, what do you think of Joseph's decision to tell his brothers about his dreams? Is it any wonder that they hated him? Do you think Joseph realized this?

    b. What administration characteristics do you see in Joseph in this passage?
    verse 2—9, 11, 12, 17
    verse 7—7
    verse 9—7, 9, 11
    verse 10—10

c. What typical problems of the gift of administration do you see exhibited in Joseph? (1, 2)

2. Turn to **Genesis 39:1–23**.

   a. In **verses 3–6**, Joseph's master saw the Lord working through Joseph, and all that he did the Lord caused to prosper. What characteristics of administration do you see in Joseph in these verses? (1, 8, 11, 16)

   b. Do you think that the administrative characteristics #3 and #12 helped him stay loyal to Potiphar and to avoid the advances of Potiphar's wife?

   c. When Joseph wouldn't commit adultery with his master's wife, and she lied to her husband about him, what do you think Joseph felt and thought?

   d. How would you have reacted if you, like Joseph, were thrown into jail unjustly? It appears that Joseph was able to trust that God would bring him through this difficulty.

   e. While he was in prison, what administrative characteristics do you see exemplified in Joseph? (1, 3, 4, 8, 11, 16)

3. Turn to **Genesis 41**.

   a. When Pharaoh called for Joseph to interpret his dream, what did Joseph tell him? In **verse 28**, what characteristic do you see here? (7)

Lesson 6 — Motive Gifts—Giving and Administration

    b. What administrative characteristics can you identify in **verses 33–36**? (2, 3, 4, 6, 7, 8, 9)

    c. It is clear, in **verses 37–40**, that Pharaoh recognized Joseph as a natural and capable leader—characteristic #16. Joseph was ready for this enormous responsibility because God had prepared him during those long, difficult years in captivity.

4. Keeping in mind Joseph's entire story, we could conclude that he had great zeal and enthusiasm for that in which he was involved—characteristic #11. Do you know anyone with this quality who might have the administrative motive gift?

5. If you have this motive gift, and you recognize in yourself some of the associated problem areas, what steps could you take to minimize these problem areas?

V. Introduction to the Motive Gift of Compassion (Mercy)

Just as servers are "doers," people with the gift of compassion are "feelers." With this gift comes pity, gentleness and forbearance. These people help others by empathizing with them and doing considerate things for them. Like givers, compassion motive people are quick to detect insincerity. They have difficulty interacting with insincere, insensitive or hard-hearted people.

Each of the motive gifts can be related to a part of the human body, to help describe the function it serves.

A. Part of the body: The *heart*—They feel and express God's love.

B. Words that describe a person with this gift include compassionate, loving, caring, helpful and obedient.

C. The Greek word for *mercy* is *eleeo* (el-eh-eh´-o), which means to show compassion by word or deed, specifically by divine grace.[3]

D. The gift of compassion can enable someone to "go the extra mile" with a person who is suffering.

Many can say, "I'm sorry you hurt." They have sympathy. Fewer can say, "I'm sorry you hurt. I'll hurt with you." They have empathy.

But the person with the motive gift of mercy can say, "I'm sorry you hurt. I'll hurt with you, and I will stay with you until you are better." They have compassion.

E. The person with the mercy motive gift is "one who shows mercy with joyous abandon."[4]

All of us can give counsel and pray, but how we give counsel and pray will differ according to our motive gift.

F. In counsel and prayer:

   1. People with a compassion motive gift can help discern areas of insensitivity in those they counsel.

   2. They feel and minister with the heart of God.

   3. People with a compassion motive gift make great intercessors.

4. They have a great desire for unity in the Body and pray accordingly.

G. In ministry:

1. People with this motive gift are great Sunday school teachers, especially in the primary age group.

2. They make very compassionate counselors, but they need to be especially aware that they can get too emotionally involved with those whom they counsel.

Each person with a motive gift can minister by leading a Bible study, but the subject, approach and desire will differ with each gift.

H. In leading a Bible study:

1. People with a compassion motive gift generally prefer using prepared materials, but they can be spontaneous in their teaching methods.

2. Their preferred focus of study is often God's love or having right relationships.

I. Related Scripture:
"This is my command: Love each other"
John 15:17.

VI. Compassion Gift Questionnaire

A. ASK PARTICIPANTS TO TURN TO THE QUESTIONNAIRE IN THE MOTIVE GIFT BOOKLET FOR THE GIFT OF COMPASSION.

PARTICIPANTS SHOULD FILL OUT THIS QUESTIONNAIRE NOW.

B. AFTER PARTICIPANTS HAVE FINISHED, *BRIEFLY* REVIEW AND DISCUSS THE CLASS MEMBERS' RESULTS.

C. ASK IF ANYONE SCORED HIGH IN THIS GIFT.

D. IT IS IMPORTANT THAT YOU ENCOURAGE EACH PARTICIPANT AS HE GETS REVELATION REGARDING HIS MOTIVE GIFT. IF YOU AGREE THAT HE HAS IDENTIFIED HIS MOTIVE GIFT, YOU MIGHT MENTION A SITUATION WHEN YOU SAW THE PARTICIPANT DISPLAY CHARACTERISTICS CONNECTED WITH THAT MOTIVE GIFT.

E. PERSONAL COMMENTS SHOULD BE ENCOURAGING, BUT NOT INVOLVE FLATTERY, AND SHOULD NOT FOCUS ON A PARTICIPANT'S FAULTS.

VII. Discussion of the Assigned Articles

ENCOURAGE THE DISCUSSION LEADER AND PARTICIPANTS TO FOCUS ON PORTIONS OF THE ARTICLE ASSIGNMENT THAT ARE IMPORTANT FOR THIS CLASS TO DISCUSS, ESPECIALLY AS IT RELATES TO THE MAIN PRINCIPLE.

VIII. Next Week's Assignment

A. REVIEW WITH THE CLASS NEXT WEEK'S ASSIGNMENT ON THE COURSE OUTLINE.

B. REVIEW THE MAIN PRINCIPLE FOR NEXT WEEK'S CLASS.

C. ASSIGN ONE PARTICIPANT TO LEAD THE BOOK DISCUSSION AND ANOTHER FOR THE ASSIGNED ARTICLE DISCUSSION FOR LESSON 7.

D. ASSIGN THE MOTIVE GIFT SCRIPTURE DISCUSSION TO A PARTICIPANT WHO IS STRONG IN THE **COMPASSION** MOTIVE GIFT. HE SHOULD ALLOT ONLY 10 MINUTES FOR HIS MOTIVE GIFT DISCUSSION. IF NO PARTICPANT SCORED HIGH IN THIS MOTIVE GIFT, THE FACILITATOR SHOULD LEAD THAT SCRIPTURE DISCUSSION.

IX. Ministry Time

A. AS FACILITATOR YOU NEED TO GUIDE THE MINISTRY TIME.

B. BE SURE TO PRAY FOR PARTICIPANTS WHO THINK THEY HAVE THE **GIVING** OR **ADMINISTRATION** MOTIVE GIFT. BELOW FIND SOME RELEVANT SCRIPTURES. AS YOU PREPARE TO MINISTER TO THESE PARTICIPANTS, ASK THE HOLY SPIRIT WHETHER YOU SHOULD PRAY FROM THESE VERSES, OR OTHERS, IN THE MINISTRY TIME,

OR PERHAPS GIVE THEM TO INDIVIDUALS AT AN APPROPRIATE TIME.

For the Giving motive gift:
"There are those who [generously] scatter abroad, and yet increase more; there are those who withhold more than is fitting or what is justly due, but it results only in want" Proverbs 11:24 (**AMP**).

"You must each decide in your heart how much to give. And don't give reluctantly or in response to pressure. 'For God loves a person who gives cheerfully.' And God will generously provide all you need. Then you will always have everything you need and plenty left over to share with others" 2 Corinthians 9:7–8 (**NLT**).

For the Administration motive gift:
"**Care for the flock that God has entrusted to you. Watch over it willingly, not grudgingly—not for what you will get out of it, but because you are eager to serve God**" 1 Peter 5:2 (**NLT**).

"And all of you, serve each other in humility, for 'God opposes the proud but favors the humble' " 1 Peter 5:5b (**NLT**).

C. ALSO, INCLUDE THE FOLLOWING IN THIS MINISTRY TIME:

Thank You, Lord, for placing this motive gift in *this person*. Show *him* how to use this gift according to Your will. Help *him* grow in maturity and understanding so that *he* can bring unity to the Body of Christ and be transformed more into the likeness of Christ.

D. NOTE: UNLESS YOU HAVE DECIDED TO WAIT UNTIL LESSON 7, THE MINISTRY EMPHASIS HAS NOW SHIFTED TO PARTICIPANTS WITH SPECIFIC MOTIVE GIFTS. ANY OTHER PERSONAL MINISTRY SHOULD NOW BE GIVEN A LOWER PRIORITY AND MAY NEED TO BE ADDRESSED AFTER CLASS.

E. INITIALLY, YOU MAY NEED TO DO THE MINISTERING, THEREBY SETTING THE EXAMPLE FOR THE CLASS.

F. AT THE BEGINNING OF THE MINISTRY TIME, REMIND PARTICIPANTS ABOUT THE FOLLOWING:

As we minister to each other, we need to recognize that we are all fine-tuning our hearing of God's voice. We may not hear clearly all the time, so we need to carefully weigh any word of prophecy a class member gives us. The following is a helpful guideline:

If it doesn't make sense, put it on the shelf. If it contradicts what God has told you, let it drop. If your spirit confirms it, make a note of it in your journal and watch God bring it about.

G. ENCOURAGE HANDS-ON MINISTRY BY CLASS MEMBERS. ALLOW THE GIFTS OF THE SPIRIT TO MANIFEST IN DIFFERENT PEOPLE.

H. CLOSE WITH PRAYER.

IN CHRIST

LESSON 7

COMPASSION MOTIVE GIFT

MAIN PRINCIPLE

People with the compassion motive gift perform the function of the heart of the body of Christ. Each of the motive gifts reveals to the world a different aspect of God's character. When we understand each other and the way God made us, we can complete each other, not compete with each other.

WWW.ZOEMINISTRIES.ORG

LESSON 7

Compassion Motive Gift

I. Let's Get Started!

    A. WELCOME THE CLASS.

    B. OPEN WITH PRAYER.

    C. WORSHIP THE LORD.

    D. READ, OR HAVE SOMEONE READ, THE MAIN PRINCIPLE FOR TODAY'S LESSON.

II. Supporting Principles From the Book

ENCOURAGE THE DISCUSSION LEADER AND PARTICIPANTS TO FOCUS ON PORTIONS OF THE BOOK ASSIGNMENT THAT ARE IMPORTANT FOR THIS CLASS TO DISCUSS, ESPECIALLY AS IT RELATES TO THE MAIN PRINCIPLE.

III. The Biblical Motive Gift of Compassion[1]— Luke 10:25–37

FACILITATORS: PRIOR TO THIS LESSON BE SURE THAT YOU HAVE REVIEWED THE FOLLOWING LISTED VERSES AND CHARACTERISTICS. THIS WILL HELP YOU ADD TO THE COMPASSION MOTIVE GIFT DISCUSSION, IF NEEDED.

Lesson 7 — Compassion Motive Gift

ALLOW ONLY 10 MINUTES FOR THIS MOTIVE GIFT SCRIPTURE DISCUSSION. IF A HIGH-SCORING PARTICIPANT IS LEADING A DISCUSSION, REMIND HIM OF THAT TIME CONSTRAINT.

As we read this passage we can recognize that the good Samaritan had the motive gift of compassion. This gift can also be called the mercy motive gift. Turn to your test entitled **"The Gift of Compassion."**

A. What do you think about the priest walking on the side of the road away from the wounded man? After all, he was a priest and it says that the wounded man was left half dead. Did the priest have the characteristics that accompany the gift of compassion?

B. The Levite also passed him by. What does the term *Levite* imply? If you don't have the mercy motive gift, do you think you also would have avoided the wounded man?

C. Verse 33 states that when the Samaritan man walked by, he felt compassion. In this verse, what compassion characteristics do you see in the Samaritan? (1, 4, 17, 18)

D. The Samaritan poured oil and wine on the man's wounds. Some people wouldn't even want to *see* the wounds, much less treat them. He had a tremendous capacity to show love!

E. What did he do next to assist the wounded man? (**verse 35**) What other compassion characteristics do you see in **verse 35**? (5, 6, 12, 13)

F. What did Jesus tell His listeners to do? (**verse 37**) So, even if your motive gift is not the gift of compassion, you should not behave like the priest or the Levite, who walked by on the other side. We should ask God for His compassion to flow through us as we choose to help people in need of assistance. In these situations we know that it is not us, but the Holy Spirit working in us, enabling us to have more compassion toward people.

G. If you have this motive gift, and you recognize in yourself some of the associated problem areas, what steps could you take to minimize these problem areas?

IV. Discussion of the Class Article "Summary of Motive Gifts"

REFER PARTICIPANTS TO THE ARTICLE **"SUMMARY OF MOTIVE GIFTS"** FOUND IN THE APPENDIX AT THE BACK OF THEIR STUDY GUIDE. SAY, "This article contains much of the material we shared with you as we taught about each gift."

ASK SOMEONE TO READ THE BRIEF SUMMARY OF EACH MOTIVE GIFT IN BOLD TYPE.

V. Supporting Principles From Scripture—Romans 12:1–21

A. Romans 12:1–8

1. Like Jesus, we are called to be living sacrifices, to die to our own selfish interests and serve God (**verses 1–2**).

Lesson 7 — Compassion Motive Gift

2. Each of the motive gifts reveals to the world a different aspect of God's character. This revelation of God comes through the body of Christ by the grace the Lord gives each one of us.
What characteristics of God might be shown through someone with the motive gift of perception? Serving? Teaching? Exhortation? Giving? Administration? Compassion?

In these gifts, we show the world and each other His holiness, His humility and willingness to serve, His truth, His desire for the best for each of His children (their personal growth and optimal usefulness), His generosity, His authority and love of order, and His mercy (**verses 3–8**).

> Jesus has all the motive gifts and is the ultimate revelation of God the Father. Similarly, as the body of Christ functions together according to God's design, we reveal God's character to others.

3. There is additional, specific advice for some of the motive gifts. For those with the prophecy motive—we are to prophesy in proportion to our faith. For those with the giving motive—we are to give generously. For those with the administration motive—we are to govern diligently. For those with the mercy motive—we are to show mercy cheerfully (**verses 6–8**).

B. Romans 12:9–21

1. Verses 9–21 are not specific to any motive gift, but are requirements for all of us in the body of Christ.

These are guidelines for serving God and showing His love to others.

2. We should not restrict our serving God and showing His love to others to our motive gifts alone. For example, if you don't have a motive gift of teaching, you still need to teach your children about God.

    a. We all should distinguish good from evil and cling to the good—not just those with the gift of prophecy (**verse 9**).

    b. We all should have a servant's heart and honor others above ourselves—not just those with the gift of serving (**verse 10**).

    c. We all should share what we have with each other—not just those with the gift of giving (**verse 13**).

    d. We all should empathize with and help others—not just those with the gift of mercy (**verses 15, 20**).

3. These verses describe the appropriate mindset the Christian should have as he serves God within his motive gift. Ask the class to list the characteristics of this mindset, using these verses. (Loving, joyful, patient, filled with faith, etc.)

VI. Final Comments on Motive Gifts

A. Obstacles in Discovering Motive Gifts

Lesson 7 — Compassion Motive Gift

1. Inadequate teaching

    a. We may not have been taught this information from **Romans 12**. (This is an example of the truth in **Hosea 4:6—"My people are destroyed from lack of knowledge."**)

    b. We may have heard confusing teaching about the gifts. Many consolidate all the gifts and callings instead of examining the groups of gifts separately.

2. Imitating the motive gifts of other people

    a. Our understanding of our true self can be clouded when we covet or imitate the gift of another person.

    b. A poor self-image can keep us from totally embracing our God-given gifting.

    c. Sometimes we try to fit into a "good Christian" mold. We think we ought to act or think in a specific way.

3. Confusion of one's motive gift with a ministry gift

    A person's *motive gift* remains constant, while the *spiritual gifts* (nine gifts of the Holy Spirit) and one's *office* (five-fold ministries) fluctuate by the calling of God.
    For example, an exhorter will always stand on the foundation of the gift of exhortation, whether he is called to be a teacher, evangelist or pastor.

How To Hear God's Voice—In Christ

4. An unteachable heart

   Being unteachable will hinder any work the Holy Spirit desires to perform in us and stops all growth!

5. Double-mindedness

   Walking with worldly standards into a Christian setting can bring confusion.

B. Discussion of "Reasons For Close Scores"

REVIEW WITH THE CLASS THE SECTION OF THE MOTIVE GIFT BOOKLET ENTITLED **"REASONS FOR CLOSE SCORES."**

Keep in mind that at certain times God may have us doing a specific type of ministry that will cause us to be stronger in an area other than our main motive gift.

C. Discussion of "Tie Breakers"

1. ASK IF THIS SECTION OF THE MOTIVE GIFT BOOKLET IS HELPFUL TO ANYONE.

2. ASK IF ANY PARTICIPANTS NEEDS HELP DETERMINING THEIR MOTIVE GIFTS.

D. Discussion of "Clarifying Close Scores"

REVIEW WITH THE CLASS THE SECTION OF THE MOTIVE GIFT BOOKLET ENTITLED **"CLARIFYING CLOSE SCORES."** ENCOURAGE THE PARTICIPANTS TO SHARE

WITH THE CLASS WHAT THEY THINK THEIR PRIMARY MOTIVE GIFT IS.

E. Develop and Exercise Your Motive Gift!

1. Learn to walk in the Spirit (**Galatians 5:25**). As we yield our giftings to the Lord, He will increase them for His glory.

2. Know the characteristics and problem areas of your motive gift and ask the Lord to show you how to use it to the fullest extent.

3. Be a servant! Be involved in a ministry that exercises your gift.

God placed us together to complete each other, not compete with each other.

F. Conclusion

1. Each gift is needed to complete the body of Christ. There should be no "lone rangers" because we need each other to accomplish the task to which God has called us. When we understand each other and the way God made us, we will truly know how God meant us to work together.

2. READ THE FOLLOWING PASSAGE ALOUD.

As each of you has received a gift (a particular spiritual talent, a gracious divine endowment), employ it for one another as [befits] good trustees of God's many-sided grace [faithful

stewards of the extremely diverse powers and gifts granted to Christians by unmerited favor].

Whoever speaks, [let him do it as one who utters] oracles of God; whoever renders service, [let him do it] as with the strength which God furnishes abundantly, so that in all things God may be glorified through Jesus Christ (the Messiah). To Him be the glory and dominion forever and ever (through endless ages). Amen (so be it). 1 Peter 4:10–11 (AMP)

VII. Discussion of the Assigned Article

ENCOURAGE THE DISCUSSION LEADER AND PARTICIPANTS TO FOCUS ON PORTIONS OF THE ARTICLE ASSIGNMENT THAT ARE IMPORTANT FOR THIS CLASS TO DISCUSS, ESPECIALLY AS IT RELATES TO THE MAIN PRINCIPLE.

VIII. Next Week's Assignment

A. REVIEW NEXT WEEK'S ASSIGNMENT ON THE COURSE OUTLINE.

B. REVIEW THE MAIN PRINCIPLE FOR LESSON 8.

C. **IMPORTANT!** SAY TO CLASS MEMBERS, The best way to digest **John 14, 15** and **16** is to fill out the study help **"The Holy Spirit—Who Is He?"** found in your Study Guide.

Lesson 7 — Compassion Motive Gift

D. ASSIGN ONE OR TWO PARTICIPANTS TO LEAD THE BOOK DISCUSSION FOR LESSON 8. FACILITATORS WILL LEAD THE DISCUSSION OF THE SCRIPTURES

IX. Ministry Time

A. AS FACILITATOR YOU NEED TO GUIDE THE MINISTRY TIME.

B. IF YOU HAVE TAKEN THE OPTION OF WAITING UNTIL LESSON 7 TO MINISTER TO PARTICIPANTS RELATED TO THEIR MOTIVE GIFTS, DO SO NOW. OTHERWISE BE SURE TO PRAY FOR PARTICIPANTS WHO THINK THEY HAVE THE **COMPASSION** MOTIVE GIFT TODAY. BELOW FIND SOME RELEVANT SCRIPTURES. AS YOU PREPARE TO MINISTER TO THESE PARTICIPANTS, ASK THE HOLY SPIRIT WHETHER YOU SHOULD PRAY FROM THESE VERSES, OR OTHERS, IN THE MINISTRY TIME, OR PERHAPS GIVE THEM TO INDIVIDUALS AT AN APPROPRIATE TIME.

For the Compassion motive gift:
"**Have mercy on me so that I may live. I love your teachings**" **Psalm 119:77 (NCV).**

"**Therefore, as God's chosen people, holy and dearly loved, clothe yourselves with compassion, kindness, humility, gentleness and patience**" **Colossians 3:12 (NIV).**

C. ALSO PRAY FOR THOSE (WITHOUT THE COMPASSION MOTIVE GIFT) WHO THIS WEEK

HAVE FINALLY IDENTIFIED THEIR GIFTS, AS WELL AS ANYONE WHO HAS NOT YET IDENTIFIED HIS MOTIVE GIFT. INCLUDE THE FOLLOWING IN THIS MINISTRY TIME:

Thank You, Lord, for placing this motive gift in *this person*. Show *him* how to use this gift according to Your will. Help *him* grow in maturity and understanding so that *he* can bring unity to the Body of Christ and be transformed more into the likeness of Christ.

D. NOTE: THE MINISTRY EMPHASIS HAS NOW SHIFTED TO PARTICIPANTS WITH SPECIFIC MOTIVE GIFTS. ANY OTHER PERSONAL MINISTRY SHOULD NOW BE GIVEN A LOWER PRIORITY AND MAY NEED TO BE ADDRESSED AFTER CLASS.

E. AT THE BEGINNING OF THE MINISTRY TIME, REMIND PARTICIPANTS ABOUT THE FOLLOWING:

As we minister to each other, we need to recognize that we are all fine-tuning our hearing of God's voice. We may not hear clearly all the time, so we need to carefully weigh any word of prophecy a class member gives us. The following is a helpful guideline:

If it doesn't make sense, put it on the shelf. If it contradicts what God has told you, let it drop. If your spirit confirms it, make a note of it in your journal and watch God bring it about.

F. ENCOURAGE HANDS-ON MINISTRY BY CLASS MEMBERS. ALLOW THE GIFTS OF THE SPIRIT TO MANIFEST IN DIFFERENT PEOPLE.

G. CLOSE WITH PRAYER.

IN CHRIST

LESSON 8

GETTING ACQUAINTED WITH THE HOLY SPIRIT

MAIN PRINCIPLE

An exciting and fulfilling relationship with the Holy Spirit is available to all believers. We are called into a deeper realm of God through daily communion with the Holy Spirit. It is out of a relationship with Him that God will pour out His powerful love on a hurting world.

LESSON 8

Getting Acquainted with the Holy Spirit

I. Let's Get Started!

   A. WELCOME THE CLASS.

   B. OPEN WITH PRAYER.

   C. WORSHIP THE LORD.

   D. INFORM THE CLASS THAT ZOE MINISTRIES IS A NON-PROFIT ORGANIZATION, WHICH DEPENDS ON DONATIONS TO ACCOMPLISH THE TASK GOD HAS GIVEN US. CLASS FEES GENERATE LITTLE OR NO PROFIT. ASK THEM TO PRAYERFULLY CONSIDER SUPPORTING ZOE. MAKE AVAILABLE ENVELOPES AND/OR DONATION CARDS.

   E. READ, OR HAVE SOMEONE READ, THE MAIN PRINCIPLE FOR TODAY'S LESSON.

II. Supporting Principles From the Book

   ENCOURAGE THE DISCUSSION LEADER AND PARTICIPANTS TO FOCUS ON PORTIONS OF THE BOOK ASSIGNMENT THAT ARE IMPORTNAT FOR THIS CLASS TO DISCUSS, ESPECIALLY AS IT RELATES TO THE MAIN PRINCIPLE.

Lesson 8 — Getting Acquainted with the Holy Spirit

III. Supporting Principles From Scripture—John 14, 15 and 16

ASK THE CLASS TO REFER TO **"THE HOLY SPIRIT—WHO IS HE?"** THE FACILITATOR'S VERSION OF THIS ARTICLE IS FOUND BELOW.

YOU MAY WANT TO INCLUDE THE FOLLOWING QUOTE FROM *THE ENCYCLOPEDIA OF 7700 ILLUSTRATIONS* AS PREPARATION FOR THE DISCUSSION OF THE ARTICLE:

> An American with an English gentleman was viewing the Niagara whirlpool rapids when he said to his friend: "Come and I'll show you the greatest unused power in the world." And taking him to the foot of Niagara Falls, "There," he said, "is the greatest unused power in the world!"
>
> "Ah no, my brother, not so!" was the reply. "The greatest unused power in the world is the Holy Spirit of the living God!"[1] A.J. Gordon

GO OVER THE STUDY HELP, SHARING ADDITIONAL INFORMATION FOUND BELOW. INVOLVE THE CLASS BY ASKING WHAT THEY WROTE ON THEIR STUDY HELPS, AND HAVE PARTICPANTS TAKE TURNS READING THE LAST SECTION.

Facilitator's Version of the Study Help "The Holy Spirit—Who Is He?"

A. The Holy Spirit at Creation

Genesis 1:1 says, **"In the beginning God created."** In Hebrew *God* is translated *Elohim* (eh-lo´-heem). "*El*" means Mighty God and "*him*" means three or more.[2] How the Father, Son and Holy Spirit worked together at creation is not completely clear. However, we know that They were all present and involved.

1. <u>God the Father</u> was present. **Acts 17:24 "The God who made the world and everything in it is the Lord of heaven and earth…."**

2. <u>Jesus</u> was present. See **John 1:1–3** and **Colossians 1:16–17: "All things were created by him and for him."**

3. <u>The Holy Spirit</u> was present. **Genesis 1:2–3 "Now the earth was formless and empty, darkness was over the surface of the deep, and the Spirit of God was hovering over the waters. And God said, 'Let there be light,' and there was light."**

    a. In **Genesis 1:2** the *hovering* action of the Holy Spirit at creation is translated as "to brood."[3] A mother hen is said to brood when she sits on her eggs to hatch them and later covers her young with her wings. The Holy Spirit hovered over the surface of the deep like a mother hen hovers over her chicks. His personality is tender, nurturing and protective.

    b. The Holy Spirit hovered over the formless earth, working together with the other Persons of the Trinity to bring into being the heavens and the earth.

Lesson 8 — Getting Acquainted with the Holy Spirit

B. The Holy Spirit in the New Testament

1. <u>He authored the Scriptures</u>. **2 Peter 1:21** Men who spoke the prophecies in the Bible were **"carried along by the Holy Spirit."**

2. <u>In the life of Jesus</u>

   a. **Luke 1:35** Jesus was conceived by the Holy Spirit.
   b. **Luke 2:40 "And the Child grew and became strong . . .."**
   c. **Luke 3:21–22** Jesus was baptized by the Holy Spirit.
   d. **Luke 4:1, 14** Jesus was controlled by the Holy Spirit.

3. <u>Jesus promised the Holy Spirit and taught these truths about Him</u>.

   a. **John 14:16–17** Jesus would send the Holy Spirit.
   b. **John 14:16** He will never leave us.
   c. **John 14:17** He leads us into all truth.
   d. **John 14:17** The world at large cannot recognize Him.
   e. **John 14:17** He lives with us and in us.
   f. **John 14:26** He teaches us.
   g. **John 14:26; 15:26** He reminds us of Jesus' words.
   h. **John 15:26** He is the source of *all* truth.
   i. **John 16:8** He convinces us of sin, the availability of God's goodness and the certainty of God's judgment.
   j. **John 16:13** He gives insight into future events.
   k. **John 16:14** He brings glory to Christ.

4. <u>After His resurrection Jesus again promised the Holy Spirit</u>.

   a. **Luke 24:49** He would send what the Father had promised.
   b. **Acts 1:4, 5, 8** The Holy Spirit was the gift the Father promised, who would give them power when He came upon them.

5. <u>The Holy Spirit was sent after Jesus ascended into heaven</u>.

   a. **Acts 2:1–4** At Pentecost each of the believers was filled with the Holy Spirit.
   b. **Acts 5:32** The Holy Spirit was given to those who obeyed God.
   c. **Acts 7:55; 11:24; 19:6** The Holy Spirit enabled believers to do amazing things for God.

C. The Holy Spirit's Role in Our Lives

1. **John 14:16** He acts as our Counselor.
2. **John 14:17** He lives with us and in us.
3. **John 14:26** He teaches us.
4. **John 16:8** He convicts us of sin.
5. **John 16:13** He guides us.
6. **John 16:14–15** He reveals Christ to us. "**…For He shall receive of Mine, and shall disclose it to you. All things that the Father has are Mine; therefore I said, that He takes of Mine, and will disclose it to you**" (NAS).

D. The Holy Spirit is a Person! He is to us as Christ was to the disciples.

1. **Ephesians 4:30** He has emotions, e.g., He grieves.

2. **Romans 8:27** He has a mind.
3. **1 Corinthians 12:11** He has a will.

E. The Holy Spirit Brings Christ Glory—John 16:14

1. He is the Spirit of Truth, just as Jesus is the truth (**John 14:6**).
2. He reminds us of Jesus' words.
3. He is the vehicle that the Father uses to tell us the things that are on His heart.
4. He makes us more like Jesus.
5. He brings us into true worship.
6. He desires that we give our praise to Jesus.

Because of Jesus' shed blood at Calvary, we now have direct access into the presence of God the Father. Because of the Holy Spirit, we can walk (**Galatians 5:25**), talk (**John 10:27**), and move in the same power Jesus had when He walked the earth (**Luke 24:47–49**).

IV. Next Week's Assignment

A. REVIEW WITH THE CLASS NEXT WEEK'S ASSIGNMENT ON THE COURSE OUTLINE.

B. REVIEW THE MAIN PRINCIPLE FOR NEXT WEEK'S CLASS.

C. ASSIGN ONE OR TWO PARTICIPANTS TO LEAD THE DISCUSSION OF THE ASSIGNED ARTICLES FOR LESSON 9. A FACILITATOR WILL TEACH ON THE PERSONS OF THE TRINITY, AS WELL AS COVER THE **"TRINITY DIAGRAM."**

V. Ministry Time

A. AS FACILITATOR YOU NEED TO GUIDE THE MINISTRY TIME.

B. IF YOU SENSE THE NEED FOR PERSONAL PRAYER MINISTRY IN A CLASS MEMBER, ASK THE PERSON CONCERNED IF HE WOULD LIKE PRAYER.

C. AT THE BEGINNING OF THE MINISTRY TIME REMIND PARTICIPANTS ABOUT THE FOLLOWING:

As we minister to each other, we need to recognize that we are all fine-tuning our hearing of God's voice. We may not hear clearly all the time, so we need to carefully weigh any word of prophecy a class member gives us. The following is a helpful guideline:

If it doesn't make sense, put it on the shelf. If it contradicts what God has told you, let it drop. If your spirit confirms it, make a note of it in your journal and watch God bring it about.

D. ENCOURAGE HANDS-ON MINISTRY BY CLASS MEMBERS. ALLOW THE GIFTS OF THE SPIRIT TO MANIFEST IN DIFFERENT PEOPLE.

E. BE CAREFUL THAT ONE PERSON DOES NOT DOMINATE THE MINISTERING.

F. CLOSE WITH PRAYER.

IN CHRIST

LESSON 9

THE INTIMACY OF THE TRINITY

MAIN PRINCIPLE

We need to get to know who the Holy Spirit is and how He works together with the Father and with Jesus. Then we can draw closer to Him and cooperate with Him as He works through us to bring glory to God.

WWW.ZOEMINISTRIES.ORG

LESSON 9

The Intimacy of the Trinity

I. Let's Get Started!

   A. WELCOME THE CLASS.

   B. OPEN WITH PRAYER.

   C. WORSHIP THE LORD.

   D. READ, OR HAVE SOMEONE READ, THE MAIN PRINCIPLE FOR TODAY'S LESSON.

II. The Holy Spirit's Role and Relationships Within the Trinity

REFER THE CLASS TO THE **"OUTLINE TO ACCOMPANY THE TRINITY TEACHING"** IN THE STUDY GUIDE TO HELP THEM BETTER FOLLOW THE TEACHING. NOTICE THAT THE NUMBERING IN THE TEACHING NOTES BELOW MATCHES THE NUMBERING ON THE PARTICIPANTS' ARTICLE. INVOLVE THE CLASS BY HAVING PARTICIPANTS READ SOME VERSES ALOUD.

I. Introduction

Most of the principles that God has given ZOE are based upon having a relationship with God. The deepening of that relationship is facilitated by an understanding of the wonderful work of the Holy Spirit, His relationship with the other two Persons of the Trinity, and how They work together.

A. **Galatians 5:25 says, "Since we live by the Spirit, let us keep in step with the Spirit."**

   1. The word for *live* in Greek is *zao* (dzah´-o), which means to be sustained in life. This new divine life resident in our beings is supplied by the Holy Spirit.[1]

   2. In the *King James Version* it reads, **"let us also walk in the Spirit."** The word for *walk* in Greek is *stoicheo* (stoy-kheh´-o), which means "walk in line with; march in battle order; fall into line."[2] To walk in the Spirit is to walk along the path He lays down for us.

It's easy to switch from walking in the Spirit to walking in the flesh. Yet when we stay on the path that the Holy Spirit lays down for us, we will see fruit in our lives.

B. **Psalm 37:23 in *The New King James Version* reads, "The steps of a good man are ordered by the Lord, and He delights in his way."**

The Holy Spirit delights in ordering our steps as we seek to serve the Lord. All we need is to get in touch with Him and find out where He wants us to walk.

Following is a story about D.L. Moody, a well-known evangelist and author. It illustrates what a relationship with the Holy Spirit can mean.

There were two women in Moody's church who had been praying for him. They prayed that Moody might understand the fullness of the Holy Spirit. Not long afterwards he had an encounter with the Holy Spirit. This is what he said about it:

> I can go back almost twenty years and remember two holy women who used to come to my meetings. It was delightful to see them there. When I began to preach I could tell by the expression of their faces that they were praying for me. At the close of the Sunday evening meetings they would say to me, "We have been praying for you." I said, "Why don't you pray for the people?" They answered, "You need the power." "I need power?" I said to myself. "Why, I thought I had the power." I had a large Sabbath school and the largest congregation in Chicago. There were some conversions at that time. I was, in a sense, satisfied.
>
> But right along these two godly women kept praying for me, and their earnest talk about "anointing for special service" set me thinking. I asked them to come and talk with me, and we got down on our knees. They poured out their hearts that I might receive the anointing from the Holy Spirit, and there came a hunger into my soul. I did not know what it was. I began to cry as I never did before. The hunger increased. I really felt that I did not want to live any longer if I could not have this power for service…
>
> Then one day in the city of New York—ah, what a day! I cannot describe it; I seldom refer to it; it is almost too sacred an experience to name…I can only say that God revealed himself to me, and I had such an experience of his love that I had to ask him to stay his hand. I went to preaching again. The sermons were not different; I did not present any new truths, and yet hundreds were converted.
>
> I would not now be placed back where I was before that blessed experience….[3]

Lesson 9 — The Intimacy of the Trinity

> As we walk obediently with the guidance of the Holy Spirit, the powerful work of the Spirit through us will transform lives.

II. In the Beginning

If we are going to discuss the Holy Spirit and the Trinity, we need to first look at the Trinity as a whole.

A. The Trinity Created the Heavens and the Earth.

Genesis 1:1–3 says, "In the beginning God created the heavens and the earth. Now the earth was formless and empty, darkness was over the surface of the deep, and the Spirit of God was hovering over the waters. And God said, 'Let there be light,' and there was light."

The word *created*, translated from the Hebrew word *bara* (baw-raw´), means to create something out of nothing.[4] God brought the heavens and the earth into existence from nothing.

The word *God* in this verse is translated from the Hebrew word *Elohim* (eh-lo´-heem). This means "the Almighty God, Creator" and is an impersonal, non-relational name for God. This word indicates a plurality of three or more.[5] As we learned in the last lesson, each Person of the Trinity was present at creation.

1. God the Father was present.
   Acts 17:24 says, "The God who made the world and everything in it is the Lord of heaven and earth...."

2. Jesus was present.
   All things were made through Jesus, who was with God the Father in the beginning (**John 1:1–3; Colossians 1:16–17**).

3. The Holy Spirit was present.
   Genesis 1:2 reads, "Now the earth was formless and empty, darkness was over the surface of the deep, and the Spirit of God was hovering over the waters."

   a. The Hebrew word for *spirit* is *ruwach* (roo´-akh), which is also the word for *breath* or *wind*.[6] The Holy Spirit can exert a driving force, which, like the wind or breath, cannot be seen.

   b. At creation the Holy Spirit hovered over the waters. One meaning of *hover* is "to brood."[7] A mother hen is said to brood when she sits on her eggs to hatch them and later covers her young with her wings. This reveals that the Holy Spirit operates in a tender, nurturing and protective way.

   c. At creation we see God speaking and the Holy Spirit then moving to bring form to the universe.

B. Mankind—God's Special Creation.

1. Man's Position

   a. **Genesis 1:26 reads, "Then God said, 'Let us make man in our image, in our likeness….' "** **"Let us"** and **"in our likeness"** indicates that the whole Trinity had a hand in creating mankind.

b. Being made in God's image indicates that God has actually imprinted His own image into us. After God made mankind, He saw that **"it was very good" Genesis 1:31**.

c. God created the heavens and the earth with His word. As God created the heavens and the earth He said, **"Let there be…."**

But in creating man, God said, **"Let us make man" (Genesis 1:26)**. **Genesis 2:7** says that God **"formed the man from the dust of the ground."** Man was created by God's own hands, as well as by His word.

d. **Genesis 2:7** also says, **"The Lord God… breathed into his nostrils the breath of life, and the man became a living being."** The word *breath* here is translated from the same Hebrew word *ruwach* (roo´-akh), which we know also means *spirit*. God breathed His very life and Spirit into mankind.

e. God created mankind to have fellowship with Him. God placed man and woman in the Garden of Eden, where He enjoyed close fellowship with them.

2. Man's Fall

a. In **Genesis 2:16–17** God said to Adam, **"You are free to eat from any tree in the garden; but you must not eat from the tree of the knowledge of good and evil, for when you eat of it you will surely die."**

So later, when Adam and Eve ate from the tree of the knowledge of good and evil, they died spiritually. They willingly separated themselves from God, and the pure, sinless type of relationship they had with Him ended, not only for them but for all mankind.

b. **Genesis 3:8–10** says, **"Then the man and his wife heard the sound of the Lord God as he was walking in the garden in the cool of the day, and they hid from the Lord God among the trees of the garden. But the Lord God called to the man, 'Where are you?' He answered, 'I heard you in the garden, and I was afraid because I was naked; so I hid.'"**

- Adam and Eve had spent so much time with God that when God came to them, they recognized His footsteps. They recognized God's voice as well—even after they sinned.

- Certainly God knew where they were. He is constantly saying to His children, "Where are you? I want to fellowship with you."

c. God told Adam and Eve that they could no longer stay in the Garden of Eden. Because of their sin He made the first animal sacrifice, to create coverings for them (**Genesis 3:21**).

d. So generations later, in **Genesis 6:5–6** it says, **"The Lord saw how great man's wickedness on the earth had become, and that every inclination of the thoughts of his heart was only evil all the time. The Lord was grieved that he had made man on the earth, and his** heart was filled with pain." Man's sin, and the subsequent separation from God, caused God much pain.

A few chapters earlier God created man and said that it was **"very good."** But now God grieved because He had made man.

III. God Reveals More of Himself

A. Elohim

At creation God was recognized as *Elohim*, Almighty God and Creator (**Genesis 1:1**). This is an impersonal, non-relational name for the Lord.

B. YHWH—"I AM WHO I AM"

All around the world people are now purposely separating themselves from God. Yet God still longs for the intimate relationship He originally had with Adam and Eve, with all *His children. And to those who are devoted to Him and desire more intimacy with Him, God is pouring out more of Himself.*

1. In the book of **Exodus** we find God revealing Himself further through a new name. At this point God was still yearning for mankind to draw near to Him. He looked for people with whom He could have fellowship.

   God found Abraham, whose descendants became the tribes of Israel, the people to whom God would make Himself known. Abraham's descendants traveled to Egypt because of a severe famine, and they eventually became slaves to Pharaoh.

2. In **Exodus 3** God chose Moses to free His people from bondage. Moses, feeling inadequate, asked God whom he should say had sent him. God responded to Moses' fear and revealed His identity as never before. God replied, **"I AM WHO I AM. This is what you are to say to the Israelites: 'I AM has sent me to you' "** Exodus 3:14.

Not only was God *Elohim*, the Mighty Creator, but now He revealed Himself in a more personal way as I AM WHO I AM, or *Yahweh* in Hebrew.

3. *Yahweh* - I AM WHO I AM means the God who is dependent on no one for His existence, because all life is contained in Him. He is the unchanging, covenant-keeping God who remains faithful to His word.[8] He keeps His covenant with His people *to be for them whatever they need*. This name for God became so revered by the Israelites that it was not spoken out loud.

And then God went to great lengths to deliver His people from bondage so that He could have fellowship with them.

4. In **Exodus 19** and **20** after they left Egypt, God offered the Israelites the chance to be His **"treasured possession"** and to come into His presence, but they declined. So, God appointed the Levites as priests, to offer sacrifices to atone for Israel's sins. Once a year the High Priest would go

Lesson 9 — The Intimacy of the Trinity

into the Holy of Holies with the blood of a lamb that was "without defect or blemish."

5. God's original plan was that we would have intimate fellowship with Him. But mankind chose to separate themselves from God; they chose to take another path. And even when God set this nation apart for Himself and He said, "You are my chosen people. I want to have fellowship with you," the Israelites said, "No." They preferred to relate to God from afar.

IV. Jesus, the Lamb

A. The Atoning Sacrifice

1. However, God had His eye on the future even as early as **Genesis 3:15** when He said to the serpent, **"And I will put enmity between you and the woman, and between your offspring and hers; he will crush your head, and you will strike his heel."** Already God had a redemptive plan to send His Son.

This is the position of many people today. They would rather relate to God from afar because they are not willing to pay the price of drawing closer.

---

2. The following quotation comes from the book *Encyclopedia of 7700 Illustrations*:

    There is in Paris a famous picture by Zwiller called "The First Night Outside Paradise." Our first parents have been driven out of the Garden of Eden and are preparing to spend the first night in the desert beyond. In the distance can be discerned the figure of the angel with the flaming sword, but the eyes of the exiles are not fixed on him. They are gazing far above his head, and there, outlined in light—faint, but unmistakable—the artist has painted a cross. In wondering awe their gaze is fastened on it.

Leslie Weatherhead[9]

Zwiller created out of **Genesis 3:15** a picture of what Christ was going to do in the future. Even then God made a provision for us to come into His presence through the cross. God is always looking for people who desire fellowship with Him.

3. Jesus came to earth for many reasons. He came that we might have eternal life. He came to redeem us from the pit of hell. He came so that we might be able to come to the Father. But most of all, Jesus came to earth out of obedience and His love for the Father, because His Father asked that of Him. Jesus came willingly, knowing that He would be the sacrificial Lamb.

4. Because of God's love for us and His desire to have fellowship with us, God sent His Son Jesus. **John 3:16–18** says, **"For *God so loved the world* that he gave his one and only Son, that whoever believes in him shall not perish but have eternal life. For God did not send his Son into the world to condemn the world, but to save the world through him. Whoever believes in him is not condemned, but whoever does not believe stands condemned already because he has not believed in the name of God's one and only Son."**

Lesson 9 — The Intimacy of the Trinity

5. In **John 1:29** John the Baptist said of Jesus, **"Look, the Lamb of God, who takes away the sin of the world!"**

6. **1 John 4:9–10** says, **"This is how God showed his love among us: He sent *his one and only Son* into the world that we might live through him. This is love: not that we loved God, but that *he loved us and sent his Son* as an atoning sacrifice for our sins."**

7. As far back as **Isaiah 53:7,12b** it was prophesied that Jesus would come and die without protest: **"He was led like a lamb to the slaughter, and as a sheep before her shearers is silent, so he did not open his mouth . . . For he bore the sin of many, and made intercession for the transgressors."**

B. Jesus' Relationship

1. With the Father

   a. We get a glimpse of Jesus' relationship with the Father in **Matthew 3:16–17**, when Jesus was baptized in the Jordan River. It says, **"As soon as Jesus was baptized, he went up out of the water. At that moment heaven was opened, and he saw the Spirit of God descending like a dove and lighting on him. And a voice from heaven said, 'This is my Son, whom I love; with Him I am well pleased.' "**

   b. Jesus' relationship with the Father is amazing; Jesus is always in submission to the Father. While

Jesus was on earth, He looked to the Father for guidance in every situation, Jesus said:

- "…The Son can do nothing by himself; he can only do what He sees his Father doing…" John 5:19.

At the beginning of Jesus' ministry we again see the Trinity clearly present. The Holy Spirit came down on Jesus in the form of a dove immediately before the Father expressed His approval of Jesus.

- "By myself I can do nothing; I judge only as I hear, and my judgment is just, for I seek not to please myself but him who sent me" John 5:30.

- "…My teaching is not my own. It comes from him who sent me" John 7:16.

- "…I do nothing on my own but speak just what the Father has taught me" John 8:28.

c. In the Garden of Gethsemane Jesus addressed the Father as *Abba*. In **Mark 14:35–36** it says, **"Going a little farther, he fell to the ground and prayed that if possible the hour might pass from him. '*Abba*, Father,' he said, 'everything is possible for you. Take this cup from me. Yet not what I will, but what you will."** Because Jesus shed His blood at Calvary for the remission of our sins, we can enter into God's presence and address Him, not only as

Elohim or *Yahweh*, but also with the endearing term *Abba*, Father.

2. With the Holy Spirit

   a. Jesus was also completely submitted to the Holy Spirit. He was conceived and anointed by the Holy Spirit. And after His baptism Jesus was **"full of the Holy Spirit" (Luke 4:1)**. This means that He was completely filled with the Spirit; there was no room for anything else.

   b. Jesus **"was led by the Spirit in the desert"** where He fasted for 40 days and was tempted by the devil. Jesus not only fully *yielded to* the Holy Spirit; He was also *empowered by* the Holy Spirit.

      - "Jesus returned to Galilee *in the power of the Spirit*... 'The Spirit of the Lord is on me, because he has anointed me to preach good news to the poor. He has sent me to proclaim freedom for the prisoners and recovery of sight for the blind, to release the oppressed, to proclaim the year of the Lord's favor'" Luke 4:14, 18–19.

      - "...God anointed Jesus of Nazareth with the Holy Spirit and power, and how he went around doing good and healing all who were under the power of the devil, because God was with Him" Acts 10:38.

> No person of the Trinity acts independently of the others. During His self-emptying life, Jesus was an agent of the Father, who worked through Him by the Holy Spirit.

V. The Holy Spirit

A. Jesus Taught the Disciples About the Holy Spirit and His Work

In the last few weeks of His life, in **John, chapters 13–17**, Jesus taught His disciples the principles He wanted to impart into their lives. He taught them about the events that would take place, about washing each other's feet, and being a servant. But most of all, He taught them about the promised Holy Spirit.

1. In **John 14:18**, Jesus said, **"I will not leave you as orphans; I will come to you."**

2. In **John 14:16–17a**, Jesus said, **"And I will ask the Father, and he will give you another Counselor to be with you forever—the Spirit of truth."**

3. The Greek word for *Counselor* that Jesus used in **John 16:7** is *parakletos* (par-ak´-lay-tos). This term further reveals the work of the Holy Spirit. It means intercessor, consoler, advocate and comforter.[10]

> The Holy Spirit would come as *another* Counselor—someone who would take the place of Jesus, to be like Jesus was when He lived with His disciples. This would be a Person who would walk and talk with them as Jesus did.

Lesson 9 — The Intimacy of the Trinity

4. In **Acts 1:4–5, 8** Jesus told His disciples to wait for the promised Holy Spirit, who would help the disciples be Jesus' witnesses.

This name is translated differently in various Bible versions; the most common translations are Comforter, Counselor and Helper. But all these terms help us understand that the Holy Spirit is called to our side to help in the way we most need Him.

5. As we continue to develop our relationship with the Holy Spirit, we will come to know His character, personality and emotions. He is a vital part of the Trinity. *He is the one who helps us become like Jesus.*

B. The Impartation of the Holy Spirit

1. Filling the Disciples

   So on the day of Pentecost (**Acts 2:1–4**) the Father sent the Holy Spirit to fill Jesus' disciples. The disciples heard Him as the sound of a violent wind. He was seen in the form of tongues of fire over each of the believers.

The Holy Spirit remains obedient to the Father and comes to fill every person who believes on the name of Jesus, claiming Him as personal Lord and Savior.

2. Symbols of the Holy Spirit

   Just as a Lamb can be a symbol for Jesus, representing His character and redemptive work, so the Holy Spirit has several symbols to represent His character and work in our lives. Remember: He is a Person—the symbols only represent His ways!

a. Wind—At Pentecost the disciples heard the Holy Spirit as a mighty wind (**Acts 2:2**). Today He still comes like wind across a threshing floor, blowing away the chaff, removing the unbelief and unholy areas in our lives.

b. Fire—At Pentecost the Holy Spirit came as tongues of fire (**Acts 2:3**). Today, the Holy Spirit comes like fire, again purifying us by burning out the dross, or impurities, in our lives. Now we need a fresh baptism of the Holy Spirit and His fire to ignite the church to become the passionate bride of Christ! That is His desire—to always point to Jesus and set aflame the heart of the bride (the Church) for her soon-coming Bridegroom!

c. Dove—At Jesus' baptism (**Matthew 3:16**) the Holy Spirit lighted upon Jesus in the form of a dove. Today the Holy Spirit comes not only in power as fire, but He also comes in gentleness like a dove.

- Like a dove, who mates for life, the Holy Spirit faithfully remains in us. He is with us as our Counselor forever.

- Doves share nesting and parental duties. The Holy Spirit works with the Father and Jesus in a nurturing way to help us grow.

- A dove's eyes allow it to see only one thing at a time. This signifies the singleness

Lesson 9 — The Intimacy of the Trinity

of purpose of the Holy Spirit (**Matthew 6:22**).[11] He focuses only on bringing glory to Jesus by making us more like Him.

- Doves express affection for each other by stroking each other and billing and cooing. The Holy Spirit speaks to us of God's love for us.

- Doves have a gentle, peaceful nature. They are non-aggressive and won't retaliate against their enemies. Our human inclination is to fight back when we are hurt. However, when we allow the Holy Spirit to be in control, He can impart His nature to us. We can ask Him, "How do I deal with this hurt?"

- The Holy Spirit will withdraw when He is grieved. He doesn't leave—because He promised never to leave us nor forsake us—but it is as if He hides His head under His wing.

3. Making Us More Like Jesus

   a. The Holy Spirit is the only part of the Trinity whose name includes the word "Holy" and His job is to make us holy. *He is the one who helps us become like Jesus.* **2 Corinthians 3:18** says, **"And we, who with unveiled faces all reflect the Lord's glory, are being transformed into his likeness with ever increasing glory, which comes from the Lord, who is the Spirit."**

   b. We cannot grow spiritual fruit without the Holy Spirit. Jesus said that He is the vine and we are the branches. As we abide in Jesus, the Holy

Spirit is the sap, the sustenance, which causes the fruit to grow in our lives.

4. Bringing Glory to Jesus the King and God the Father

   a. The Holy Spirit always guides us to worship Jesus. He helps us and brings us into true worship (**John 4:23–24**).

   b. He always directs our attention to Jesus, reminding us of what Jesus has said (**John 14:26**).

When the Spirit manifests His fruit in us, people are drawn to us. But we need to direct their praise to Jesus. We can't operate the way the Holy Spirit intends if we don't give the glory to whom it is due—to Jesus, the King of kings and Lord of lords.

---

   c. The Holy Spirit never takes glory to Himself; He gives glory to Jesus. He reveals to us that Jesus is the King of kings, who is now sitting at the right hand of the Father (**John 16:14**).

   Galatians 4:4–7 says, "But when the time had fully come, God sent his Son, born of a woman, born under law, to redeem those under law, that we might receive the full rights of sons. Because you are sons God sent the Spirit of his Son into our hearts, the Spirit who calls out, 'Abba, Father.' So you are no longer a slave, but a son; and since you are a son, God has made you also an heir."

Romans 8:15–16 says, "For you did not receive a spirit that makes you a slave again to fear, but you received the Spirit of sonship. And by him we cry, '*Abba*, Father.' "

III. Explanation of the Trinity Diagram

THE **"TRINITY DIAGRAM"** IS NOT TO BE USED DURING THE PRECEDING TEACHING. THE FOLLOWING SUMMARY IS AN EXPLANATION OF THE DIAGRAM. IT IS FOR THE FACILITATOR'S USE ONLY. YOU ARE NOT TO TEACH FROM IT, RATHER USE IT FOR YOUR PREPARATION BEFORE CLASS. AS YOU EXPLAIN THIS DIAGRAM, YOU SHOULD POINT TO EACH SPECIFIC ITEM ON THE DIAGRAM AS YOU IDENTIFY IT.

Now that we have finished the teaching on the workings of the Trinity, let's turn our attention to the **"Trinity Diagram"** found in Lesson 9 of the Study Guide.

This diagram helps describe how the Trinity operates together—completing each other, rather than competing—giving place or honor to one another.

A. (POINT TO ELOHIM, GOD THE CREATOR)
Elohim is an impersonal name for God that indicates a plurality of three or more (**Genesis 1:1**). In the beginning we know that God desired to have relationship with mankind. We also know that man separated himself from God by sinning, and this deeply grieved God.

B. (POINT TO YAHWEH)

When God revealed Himself to Moses as *Yahweh,* I AM WHO I AM, He disclosed Himself as a more personal God. Then God called His people His "treasured possession" and "a kingdom of priests" but the Israelites preferred not to have the kind of relationship for which God longed.

C. Fortunately for us, God knew mankind and had a plan from the beginning. All through the Old Testament, even as early as **Genesis 3**, He pointed toward the Deliverer, the Messiah, who would come and redeem His people.

(POINT TO JESUS, THE LAMB)
Every year the High Priest would sacrifice a lamb without blemish in atonement for the sins of the Israelites. As John the Baptist saw Jesus, he said, **"Look, the Lamb of God, who takes away the sins of the world!"** **(John 1:29)**. Jesus came to die like an unblemished lamb, as an atoning sacrifice, once and for all for mankind. How precious is the Lamb, obediently coming to earth that He might die and bring us back into relationship with the Father.

D. Jesus talked about *Yahweh* and *Elohim* as His Father. He taught His disciples to refer to God as Father. He talked about the Holy Spirit whom He would send from the Father to the disciples. But before He could send the Spirit, He had to die on the cross for our sins.

(POINT TO THE CROSS)
Jesus willingly went to the cross—not defending Himself—and shed His blood that we might once again be allowed into the presence of our holy God.

Lesson 9 — The Intimacy of the Trinity

E. How much the Father loves you and me that He sent His Son.

(POINT TO THE PEOPLE)
As it says in **John 3:16**: **"God so loved the world that he gave his one and only Son, that whoever believes in him shall not perish but have eternal life."** How much Jesus loves us that He willingly died on the cross.

F. After Jesus ascended and sat at the right hand of God, He asked the Father to send the Spirit.

(POINT TO THE HOLY SPIRIT AS FIRE)
In **Acts 2** the Holy Spirit came as wind and fire to fill the disciples. The fire represents the Holy Spirit's work. His job is to burn out the impurities and unbelief from our lives. He makes us more like Christ. He wants to make us a spotless bride for Jesus. The Holy Spirit gives us the fruit of the Spirit. He allows us to minister in the gifts of the Spirit, as He wills. The Holy Spirit is to us, as Jesus was to the disciples.

G. **(POINT TO THE DOVE)**
The Holy Spirit also came as a gentle dove. We have already discussed the similarities between the characteristics of the Holy Spirit and a dove. A dove mates for life and He focuses only on one thing.

H. The Holy Spirit helps us focus on the return of Jesus, the soon-coming King.

(POINT TO THE CROWN)
The Holy Spirit living in us always points to Jesus. He is preparing us to be the bride of Christ, the King.

I. And now through Jesus' shed blood at Calvary **(POINT TO THE CROSS AGAIN)**, we can enter into God's presence, into the Holy of Holies, and address God not only as *Elohim* or *Yahweh*, but also as *Abba*, Daddy.

(POINT TO ABBA, FATHER)
Jesus called out, "*Abba*," in the Garden of Gethsemane, and the Holy Spirit enables us to cry, "*Abba*, Father."

J. Notice the arrows on the diagram. They indicate a circular motion—all because God sent His Son to die so that we might have eternal life.

   1. God looks down, through Jesus and His blood, to His children. He speaks to us with love and He desires relationship. Today we can respond to the Father's voice through the power of the Holy Spirit, bringing glory to God. We eagerly anticipate the return of our King of Kings.

   2. Again the circular motion becomes apparent. God gives honor to Jesus, Jesus gives honor to the Holy Spirit, the Holy Spirit gives honor to Jesus, and Jesus again gives honor to the Father. Jesus came to earth to do so much for mankind, but He came out of obedience and love for the Father.

   3. The Holy Spirit enables us to work together in unity with one another. When we go to prayer, we do so with the help of the Holy Spirit through the blood of the Lamb. Our cries come to the Father and He responds by speaking into our hearts. We hear Him by the power of the Holy Spirit. Many Christians fail to recognize that it is through the Holy Spirit, and a revelation of who He is in our lives, that we

can come wholeheartedly, with full authority and power, and obtain what we need from the Father.

K. As we began the teaching on the Trinity, so we end this discussion of the diagram with **Galatians 5:25: "Since we live by the Spirit, let us keep in step with the Spirit."** As the Trinity is active in our lives, we will walk in the Spirit, hearing God's voice because of the blood of the Lamb, and we will do what is on God's heart for His glory and honor. We will be the holy and blameless bride, anticipating and longing for our Bridegroom's return.

IV. Discussion of the Assigned Articles

TIME PERMITTING, ENCOURAGE THE DISCUSSION LEADER AND PARTICIPANTS TO FOCUS ON PORTIONS OF THE ARTICLE ASSIGNMENT THAT ARE IMPORTANT FOR THIS CLASS TO DISCUSS, ESPECIALLY AS IT RELATES TO THE MAIN PRINCIPLE.

V. Next Week's Assignment

A. REVIEW WITH THE CLASS NEXT WEEK'S ASSIGNMENT ON THE COURSE OUTLINE.

B. REVIEW THE MAIN PRINCIPLE FOR NEXT WEEK'S CLASS.

C. ASSIGN DISCUSSION LEADERS FOR LESSON 10: ONE PARTICIPANT TO LEAD THE BOOK DISCUSSION AND ANOTHER TO LEAD

THE ASSIGNED ARTICLE DISCUSSION. FACILITATORS WILL LEAD THE DISCUSSION OF THE SCRIPTURES.

VI. Ministry Time

A. AS FACILITATOR YOU NEED TO GUIDE THE MINISTRY TIME.

B. ASK THE PARTICIPANTS IF THEY WOULD LIKE PRAYER FOR MORE OF A RELEASE OF THE HOLY SPIRIT IN THEIR LIVES. SEE APPENDIX B FOR SOME RELEVANT SCRIPTURES YOU MIGHT WANT TO USE AS YOU PRAY FOR INTERESTED PARTICIPANTS.

C. IF YOU SENSE THE NEED FOR PERSONAL PRAYER MINISTRY IN A CLASS MEMBER, ASK THE PERSON CONCERNED IF HE WOULD LIKE PRAYER.

D. AT THE BEGINNING OF THE MINISTRY TIME REMIND PARTICIPANTS ABOUT THE FOLLOWING:

As we minister to each other, we need to recognize that we are all fine-tuning our hearing of God's voice. We may not hear clearly all the time, so we need to carefully weigh any word of prophecy a class member gives us. The following is a helpful guideline:

If it doesn't make sense, put it on the shelf. If it contradicts what God has told you, let it drop. If your spirit confirms it, make a note of it in your journal and watch God bring it about.

E. ENCOURAGE HANDS-ON MINISTRY BY CLASS MEMBERS. ALLOW THE GIFTS OF THE SPIRIT TO MANIFEST IN DIFFERENT PEOPLE.

F. BE CAREFUL THAT ONE PERSON DOES NOT DOMINATE THE MINISTERING.

G. CLOSE WITH PRAYER.

IN CHRIST

LESSON 10

GIFTS OF THE SPIRIT– REVELATION GIFTS

MAIN PRINCIPLE

*We can work together in partnership with the Holy Spirit. As we lay aside our fears and our own plans, the Holy Spirit will tell us what to do and say.
We are privileged to participate with God as His Spirit moves upon us with words of wisdom, words of knowledge and discerning of spirits.*

WWW.ZOEMINISTRIES.ORG

LESSON 10

Gifts of the Spirit–Revelation Gifts

I. Let's Get Started!

A. WELCOME THE CLASS.

B. OPEN WITH PRAYER.

C. WORSHIP THE LORD.

D. READ, OR HAVE SOMEONE READ, THE MAIN PRINCIPLE FOR TODAY'S LESSON.

II. Supporting Principles From the Book

ENCOURAGE THE DISCUSSION LEADER AND PARTICIPANTS TO FOCUS ON PORTIONS OF THE BOOK ASSIGNMENT THAT ARE IMPORTANT FOR THIS CLASS TO DISCUSS, ESPECIALLY AS IT RELATES TO THE MAIN PRINCIPLE.

III. Introduction to the Gifts of the Spirit (The Manifestation Gifts)— 1 Corinthians 12

A. In **1 Corinthians 12:8–10** we find the spiritual, or manifestation, gifts listed. HAVE SOMEONE READ **1 CORINTHIANS 12:1–11**.

You may remember the article from Lesson 3, **"Three Biblical Groups of Gifts,"** in which the three groups of gifts are outlined. Let's turn to it now. It defines the spiritual gifts as supernatural gifts that are manifestations of the Holy Spirit as He moves upon believers. These gifts are administered by the Holy Spirit for the common good, using whom He chooses, and at the time of need.

B. For the next few weeks we will be looking at each of the spiritual, or manifestation, gifts.

Just as the motive gifts can be associated with a part of the body, so it is with the gifts of the Spirit.

1. With the *revelation gifts,* the Holy Spirit moves upon your mind, causing you to *know* that you know something. We can associate the revelation gifts with the *head.*

2. With the *power gifts* the Holy Spirit moves upon you, enabling you to *do* something. In the power gifts the Holy Spirit often operates through your hands. Thus, we can associate the power gifts with the *hands.*

3. With the *vocal gifts* the Holy Spirit moves upon you, giving you something to *speak* out. We can associate the vocal gifts with the *mouth.*

C. All of these gifts enable us to continue Jesus' ministry (**John 14:12**). They are a means of spiritual growth for believers and outreach to unbelievers. Through them, believers are edified, encouraged and comforted. By these manifestation gifts, unbelievers can be convinced that God is real, and be convicted of their need for a Savior.

D. Looking at **1 Corinthians 12**, what do we need to keep in mind as we operate in the manifestation gifts?

1. We are all a part of the body of Christ, and all our gifts are necessary and important.

2. We need to allow the manifestation of a *variety* of the spiritual gifts (**verses 7–11, 28–30**). The Holy Spirit will orchestrate the use of the specific gifts needed for a gathering in order to meet the needs of the people there. It would not work to have everyone simultaneously try to be the leader, or everyone teach, prophesy or publicly speak in tongues.

3. We should never have a condescending attitude, viewing another believer as less important because he operates in a less dramatic gift or has less spiritual understanding (**verses 22–23**).

4. **Verse 31 says, "But eagerly desire the greater gifts. And now I will show you the most excellent way."** This verse leads into **chapter 13**, which expounds on love. The **"greater gifts"** could refer to those gifts that most display God's love in a specific situation. Any of the manifestation gifts could be God's chosen expression of love to someone.

IV. Supporting Principles From Scripture—
   Matthew 22:15–22
   John 4:1–42
   Acts 13:4–12

The revelation gifts—the word of wisdom, word of knowledge and discerning of spirits—are often used in conjunction with the other gifts of the Holy Spirit.

Lesson 10 — Gifts of the Spirit—Revelation Gifts

A. The Word of Wisdom

1. Definition of a *Word of Wisdom*:

   Have someone read the definition from the study help **"The Gifts of the Holy Spirit—The Revelation Gifts."**

   "A word of wisdom is not 'a' word of wisdom but 'the' word of wisdom…It is the answer or solution or the will of God in that situation."[1]

   a. We can develop a great deal of wisdom as we study the Scriptures, but a word of wisdom is not the wisdom that comes from spending time in God's Word. It is wisdom that comes directly from the Lord for use in a particular situation.

   b. This gift is listed first because we need wisdom for operating in all the other gifts of the Spirit, in ways that glorify God.

   c. Gifts of wisdom will play a phenomenal part in the Church's last days. It will be vital that we have the mind of Christ in all situations.

2. Matthew 22:15–22

   a. The Pharisees were ardent nationalists opposed to the Roman rule in Israel. The Herodians supported the Roman rule through the Herods. Here we see these historically bitter enemies plotting together to entrap Jesus (**verses 15–16**).

b. **Verse 16 reads, " 'Teacher,' they said, 'we know you are a man of integrity and that you teach the way of God in accordance with the truth.' "**

Integrity comes from the Greek word *alethes* (al-ay-thace´), which means sincere, honest, frank and genuine.[2] *Truth* comes from the Greek word *aletheia* (al-ay´-thia), which means "without pretense, falsehood, deceit; with sincerity of mind and purpose; without hypocrisy and lust for personal gain."[3]

What they said about Jesus was actually true, but they tried to use flattery to catch Jesus off guard.

c. Then they asked a question intended to entrap Him regardless of His answer. **"Is it lawful to pay taxes to Caesar, or not?" verse 17**. If Jesus answered "No," the Herodians would report Him to the Roman government and He could be executed for treason. If He answered "Yes," the Pharisees would denounce Him to the people as disloyal to His nation. He was in a seemingly hopeless situation!

d. Jesus knew **"their evil intent"** and exposed their plan, calling them **"hypocrites" verse 18.**

- Jesus *knew* what they were planning through a *word of knowledge* from the Holy Spirit.

- *Hypocrite* comes from the Greek word *hupokrites* (hoop-ok-ree-tace´), which refers to an actor, stage player, pretender or dissembler—one who conceals his real motives, nature or feelings under a pretense.[4]

e. Jesus received the *word of wisdom* in **verses 19–21.** Here Jesus received from the Holy Spirit the revelation of how to escape their trap!

f. The result of the word of wisdom is seen in **verse 22: "When they heard this they were amazed. So they left him and went away."**

C. The Word of Knowledge

1. Definition of a *Word of Knowledge:*

HAVE SOMEONE READ THE DEFINITION FROM THE STUDY HELP **"THE GIFTS OF THE HOLY SPIRIT—THE REVELATION GIFTS."**

"A word of knowledge is the supernatural revelation to man of some detail of the knowledge of God. It is the impartation of facts and information which are humanly impossible to know." The word of knowledge can reveal facts about the past, present or future, or the intent of a person's heart.[5]

---

a. The Holy Spirit reveals this specific information for the purpose of freeing individuals and the Body of Christ, bringing people into right relationship with the Father. The Holy Spirit does not reveal such things for purposes of gossiping or other misuses!

b. Often the word of knowledge is intended for use in prayer only. The Lord may call us to intercede for the situation until He gives us a release to share the information.

2. **John 4:1–42**

   a. This encounter between Jesus and the Samaritan woman is well known. During their conversation the Holy Spirit gave Jesus a word of knowledge about this woman. Jesus told her to go get her husband, knowing that she had no husband. In **verses 17–18** Jesus said, **"You are right when you say you have no husband. The fact is, you have had five husbands, and the man you now have is not your husband."**

   b. The first result of Jesus delivering this word of knowledge to the woman can be found in **verse 19**. His knowledge of this hidden fact caused her to recognize that God was working through Jesus. She called Him a prophet. In fact, she ran back to town and told the people about Jesus. She wondered, **"Could this be the Christ?" verse 29.**

   c. Many believed Jesus to be the Messiah after hearing this woman's testimony about Him (**verse 39**). Once Jesus received their undivided attention, many more people believed after hearing what He had to say (**verses 41–42**).

A word of knowledge can give servants of God credibility and can prove that God is real and active in everyday life.

Lesson 10 — Gifts of the Spirit—Revelation Gifts

E. Discerning of Spirits

1. Definition of *Discerning of Spirits:*

   HAVE SOMEONE READ THE DEFINITION FROM THE STUDY HELP **"THE GIFTS OF THE HOLY SPIRIT—THE REVELATION GIFTS."**

   "The gift of discerning of spirits is the God-given ability to perceive the presence and activity of a spirit that motivates a human being, whether good or bad. To 'discern' means to perceive, distinguish or differentiate."[6]

   a. This gift is accompanied by a God-given ability to challenge or cope with any evil spirits discerned.

   b. The placement of this gift in the list in **1 Corinthians 12** may not be coincidental. By placing the discerning of spirits between the spoken gifts, the Holy Spirit may be communicating our need for discernment with all the other gifts, but especially with vocal gifts.

   For example, in a meeting if someone shares a message that they think is from the Lord, the others present need to use discernment regarding what was prophesied. In **1 Corinthians 14:29** it reads, **"Two or three prophets should speak, and the others should weigh carefully what is said."**

   1 John 4:1 echoes this advice: **". . . Test the spirits to discover whether they are from**

God, because many false prophets have gone out into the world." We need to know whether what has been spoken is from God, the speaker's human nature or evil spirits.

c. As with all the gifts, the person acting as God's vessel with the discerning of spirits needs to have a clean heart before God. He needs to be filled with the Holy Spirit, and to spend time in prayer and the Scriptures.

2. **Acts 13:4–12**

   a. This whole encounter was preceded by Barnabas and Saul being **"sent . . . by the Holy Spirit" verse 4.**

   Barnabas and Saul were empowered missionaries. All missionaries should minister under the specific call and will of the Holy Spirit. Too often individuals go out to the mission field motivated by others, rather than with the direction and anointing of the Holy Spirit. It is only when we are this sensitive to the Holy Spirit's timing and direction that we will see results such as those found in this passage.

   b. Barnabas and Saul had been preaching all across this island. However, they met some opposition from Bar-Jesus, a Jewish sorcerer and false prophet, who served as an attendant of the proconsul. *The Living Bible* states that this man **"had *attached himself* to the governor, Sergius Paulus" verse 7.** The verb *attached* gives us a glimpse into his motivation.

c. **"But Elymas the sorcerer (for that is what his name means) opposed them and tried to turn the proconsul from the faith" verse 8.**

- According to the *Full Life Study Bible* this "sorcerer was probably a Jewish astrologer. Astrologers taught that the destiny of the individual was determined by celestial bodies. They believed they could foretell the future by examining the position of the stars and planets. All sorcery or astrology stands in opposition to the gospel of Christ because it involves Satan and the demonic."[7] (See **Acts 13:10** and **Deuteronomy 18:9–12**.)

- *Opposed* is translated from the Greek word *anthistemi* (anth-is´-tay-mee), which means to set one's self against, to resist. [8]

d. **Verses 9–10 state that Saul, "filled with the Holy Spirit, looked straight at Elymas and said, 'You are a child of the devil and an enemy of everything that is right! You are full of all kinds of deceit and trickery. Will you never stop perverting the right ways of the Lord?'"**

- Here we have what you might call a clash of the kingdoms.

- Saul, representing God's kingdom, *had* to be filled with the Holy Spirit. Repeated fillings are necessary in confronting opposition, whether it involves spreading and advancing the Gospel, or directly challenging Satan's activity.

- Jesus was led from the wilderness in the power of the Holy Spirit and began His public ministry of proclaiming that the kingdom of God was near, casting out demons, and healing the sick (**Luke 4:14**). If Jesus, the Son of God, needed such divine empowerment, should we need it any less?

We need to be refilled with the Holy Spirit on a daily basis because we "leak."

e. Verse 10 is an example of the gift of discerning of spirits. Saul exposed the true character of Elymas, using extremely strong words. To speak these words, one would need to be led by the Holy Spirit and operate in the gifts of the Spirit.

f. **Verse 11 is an example of a word of knowledge.** The Holy Spirit moved upon Saul so that he *knew* God was going to blind Elymas.

g. The result was that the sorcerer was blinded and Sergius Paulus **"believed, for he was amazed at the teaching about the Lord" verse 12.**

When the gifts of the Holy Spirit operate properly through an individual, it will not bring glory to that person. When people see the results of these gifts, Jesus will receive the glory.

Believe in this verse means to have faith in, commit to, and essentially entrust one's well-being to Christ.[9]

V. Discussion of the Assigned Articles

ENCOURAGE THE DISCUSSION LEADER AND PARTICIPANTS TO FOCUS ON PORTIONS OF THE ARTICLE ASSIGNMENT THAT ARE IMPORTANT FOR THIS CLASS TO DISCUSS, ESPECIALLY AS IT RELATES TO THE MAIN PRINCIPLE.

VI. Next Week's Assignment

A. REVIEW WITH THE CLASS NEXT WEEK'S ASSIGNMENT ON THE COURSE OUTLINE.

B. REVIEW THE MAIN PRINCIPLE FOR NEXT WEEK'S CLASS.

C. ASSIGN DISCUSSION LEADERS FOR LESSON 11: ONE PARTICIPANT TO LEAD THE BOOK DISCUSSION AND ANOTHER TO LEAD THE ASSIGNED ARTICLE DISCUSSION. FACILITATORS WILL LEAD THE DISCUSSION OF THE SCRIPTURES.

VII. Ministry Time

A. AS FACILITATOR YOU NEED TO GUIDE THE MINISTRY TIME.

B. IF YOU SENSE THE NEED FOR PERSONAL PRAYER MINISTRY IN A CLASS MEMBER, ASK THE PERSON CONCERNED IF HE WOULD LIKE PRAYER.

C. AT THE BEGINNING OF THE MINISTRY TIME, REMIND PARTICIPANTS ABOUT THE FOLLOWING:

As we minister to each other, we need to recognize that we are all fine-tuning our hearing of God's voice. We may not hear clearly all the time, so we need to carefully weigh any word of prophecy a class member gives us. The following is a helpful guideline:

If it doesn't make sense, put it on the shelf. If it contradicts what God has told you, let it drop. If your spirit confirms it, make a note of it in your journal and watch God bring it about.

D. PRAY THE FOLLOWING:

Lord, help us apply what we have learned by moving upon us with the **revelation gifts**—a word of wisdom, a word of knowledge or the discerning of spirits. We want the Holy Spirit to be free to operate through us. Reveal the operation of the Holy Spirit in these gifts, as He wills.

E. ENCOURAGE HANDS-ON MINISTRY BY CLASS MEMBERS. ALLOW THE GIFTS OF THE SPIRIT TO MANIFEST IN DIFFERENT PEOPLE.

F. BE CAREFUL THAT ONE PERSON DOES NOT DOMINATE THE MINISTERING.

G. CLOSE WITH PRAYER.

IN CHRIST

LESSON 11

GIFTS OF THE SPIRIT— POWER GIFTS

MAIN PRINCIPLE

We are privileged to participate with God as His Spirit moves upon us with the gift of faith, gifts of healing and the working of miracles.

LESSON 11

Gifts of the Spirit—Power Gifts

I. Let's Get Started!

A. WELCOME THE CLASS.

B. OPEN WITH PRAYER.

C. WORSHIP THE LORD.

D. READ, OR HAVE SOMEONE READ, THE MAIN PRINCIPLE FOR TODAY'S LESSON.

II. Supporting Principles From the Book

ENCOURAGE THE DISCUSSION LEADER AND PARTICIPANTS TO FOCUS ON PORTIONS OF THE BOOK ASSIGNMENT THAT ARE IMPORTANT FOR THIS CLASS TO DISCUSS, ESPECIALLY AS IT RELATES TO THE MAIN PRINCIPLE.

III. Supporting Principles From Scripture—
1 Corinthians 13
1 Kings 17:1–16
Matthew 20:29–34
Matthew 14:22–33

A. 1 Corinthians 13

1. In review, the manifestation gifts are gifts bestowed by the Lord when He chooses and for His purposes.

Lesson 11 — Gifts of the Spirit—Power Gifts

They are to be used to strengthen the church, bring people into a right relationship with God and to glorify Him.

2. The only power manifestation gift specifically mentioned in this chapter is the *gift of faith*. **Verse 2 mentions "faith that can move mountains."**

3. In **verses 1–3** Paul makes it clear that if we **"have not love,"** our spiritual gifts, spiritual understanding or great amount of faith are worthless. Any spiritual gift, revelation or faith we are given needs to be put into use with love. We need to ask the Holy Spirit for wisdom regarding the most helpful way to operate in the manifestation gifts.

4. When Jesus returns, all of our spiritual gifting and understanding will not matter (**verses 8–10**). The important question will be: Did we love? Did we love the Lord our God with all our heart and soul and mind, and our neighbors as ourselves (**Matthew 22:37–39**)?

B. **The Gift of Faith**

1. Definition of a *Gift of Faith*:

HAVE SOMEONE READ THE DEFINITION FROM THE STUDY HELP **"THE POWER GIFTS."**

"This is not saving faith but a special supernatural faith imparted by the Holy Spirit that enables the Christian to believe God for the extraordinary and miraculous. It is a faith that moves mountains (1 Cor. 13:2) and is often found in combination with other manifestations such as healings and miracles."[1]

a. A gift of faith is a sure knowledge that God is going to work in a specific situation. This type of faith is supernatural (above the natural). This faith gives you assurance that God will do something before you actually see Him do it.

b. Jesus taught us that this faith leaves absolutely no doubt in the heart of the one believing (**Matthew 21:21**). When you operate in a gift of faith, there is complete assurance that God will do what He has told you He will do.

c. This gift of faith may require you to speak out or pray something specific. This faith is active, not passive. For example, when you receive a gift of faith for a healing, someone will need to obey God's instructions in order to release His power to heal.

2. **1 Kings 17:1–16**

   a. In **verse 1** Elijah proclaimed God's plan to King Ahab. It required faith and courage to give the king a prediction of drought—no rain or dew for three years!

   b. "The drought was not only a divine judgment on a nation that had turned to idolatry, but also a demonstration that even though Baal was considered the god of fertility and lord of the rain clouds, he was powerless to give rain."[2]

   c. Elijah had faith that the Lord would do as He said after he gave this word to Ahab. Elijah was totally dependent upon the Lord to provide what he needed (**verses 4–5**).

Lesson 11 — Gifts of the Spirit—Power Gifts

    d. Elijah, God's faithful servant, was miraculously sustained while the Israelites were experiencing famine in the promised land (**verse 6**). Elijah was obedient to the Lord despite the circumstances, and the Lord responded to his faith by providing for him.

    e. We need to remember that when God guides us to do something, He will provide what we need to do it. Steady faith in God's direction will help us overcome fear.

    f. In **verses 7–16** we see Elijah ask a widow to give him her last bit of food. In **verse 14** the Lord had told Elijah that the widow's jar of flour and jug of oil would not be depleted. The Lord gave Elijah a gift of faith to tell this to the widow before it happened. Elijah said that if she followed his instructions, God would provide for all her needs. The woman overcame her fear and responded in faith, and God kept His promise.

A gift of faith and its positive outcome causes the faith of others to increase.

C. Gifts of Healing

    1. Definitions of *Healing:*

        a. This manifestation of the Spirit is called *gifts* of healing (plural) because it can involve different levels, kinds and methods of healing.

        b. There are different definitions of healing in the

Hebrew and Greek, in both the New and Old Testament.

- In **Exodus 15:26** God said, **"For I am the Lord who heals you."** The term *heals* is translated from the Hebrew word *rapha´* (raw-faw´), which means to heal of a disease; to mend, comfort and restore.[3] The main context in this verse is one of healing from physical disease.

- In **Malachi 4:2**, the Hebrew word *marpe´* (mar-pay´) is used. *Marpe´* refers to a wide spectrum of healing. It means the healing of a disease; the refreshing both of body and mind; deliverance and tranquility.[4]

- In **Matthew 12:22**, we find the Greek word *therapeuo* (ther-ap-yoo´-o). The literal meaning of *therapeuo* is to wait upon menially, as you would wait upon a sick person. It means to relieve of a disease or to cure.[5] In this verse Jesus healed a man who was demon-possessed, blind and mute.

- In **Matthew 9:22** and **Luke 7:50** the Greek word *sozo* (sode´-zo) is used. *Sozo* means to save, deliver, protect, heal or make whole.[6] The verses that contain the word *sozo* depict situations of healing that involve the forgiveness of sins and spiritual salvation, or the rescue of a person from disease and the problems that accompany it.

- In **Luke 5:17** the Greek word *iaomai* (ee-ah´-om-ahee) is used. *Iaomai* means to heal or cure a physical disease; to free from sin and bring about salvation; to make whole.

HAVE SOMEONE READ THE DEFINITION OF THE GIFTS OF HEALING FROM THE STUDY HELP "THE POWER GIFTS."

c. There are different levels of healing.

- Instant, as in **Matthew 8:3** and **Mark 1:31**
- Progressive, as in **Mark 8:22–25**

d. There are different kinds of healing.

- Healing of the spirit (spiritual healing—salvation, deliverance)
- Healing of the soul (healing of the mind, will or emotions)
- Healing of the body (physical healing)

e. There are different methods of healing.

- Praying and anointing with oil **(James 5:14–15)**
- Laying on of hands by a believer **(Mark 16:18)**
- The spoken word **(Luke 7:1–10)**
- Touch **(Mark 5:27–30)**
- Giving the sick instructions to follow **(Luke 17:14)**
- Others **(Acts 19:11–12)**

Often we need the operation of the revelation gifts—a message of wisdom, a message of knowledge or discerning of spirits—in order to know how to pray for healing.

---

f. Comments:

Praying, "if it be Thy will," may not be appropriate because according to God's Word, healing is God's will. We may want to pray, "Thy will be done on earth as it is in heaven" (where there is no sickness). Scriptures that support the Lord's desire to heal include:

- **Exodus 15:26**
- **Exodus 23:25**
- **Psalm 103:3**

2. **Matthew 20:29–34**

   a. Perhaps these two blind men asked Jesus for mercy because they had heard of His miracles. (**verse 30**).

   b. There is a stark contrast between the reaction of the crowd and Jesus' reaction to these men (**verses 31–32**).

   c. The blind men ignored the attempt of the crowd to deter them from crying out for mercy. Their despair reached Jesus' heart of mercy (**verses 31–32**).

   d. Jesus called to them, **"What do you want me to do for you?"** The answer is rather obvious since they were blind (**verse 32**). It is as if Jesus wanted to assess their level of faith.

   e. Their response was one of boldness, for they knew what they wanted. They spoke a prayerful statement, **"Lord, …we want our sight" verse 33.**

Lesson 11 — Gifts of the Spirit—Power Gifts

    f. Their faith-filled prayer must have been music to Jesus' ears. *Our* attitude of faith can touch Jesus' heart.

    g. Jesus' reaction to their faith-filled request was compassion. And responding to the compassion from within, Jesus touched them (**verse 34**).

Where there is divine compassion, there is power to bless in any way, shape or form. As we seek to be like Jesus, we should share in His compassion toward those who suffer.

D. A Gift of Working of Miracles

1. Definition of the *Gift of Working of Miracles:*

HAVE SOMEONE READ THE DEFINITIONS OF MIRACLE AND THE GIFT OF MIRACLES FROM THE STUDY HELP **"THE POWER GIFTS."**

"The 'gift of miracles' is simply the God-given ability to co-operate with God as He performs miracles."[8]

    a. Miracles are "deeds of supernatural power that alter the normal course of nature. They include divine acts in which God's kingdom is manifested against Satan and evil spirits."[9]

    b. The word *miracle* in **1 Corinthians 12:10 (KJV)** is related to the Greek word *dunamis* (doo´-nam-is). It speaks of God's might and miraculous power.[10]

c. The greatest miracles recorded in the Old Testament occurred through Moses, Elijah and Elisha. Jesus performed more miracles than anyone else throughout the Bible, and many of His miracles weren't even recorded, according to **John 21:25**.

2. **Matthew 14:22–33**

    a. According to **verse 23,** Jesus spent time alone in prayer that afternoon. Jesus thereby set an example for us.

    b. Jesus performed a miracle by walking on the water (**verse 25**).

If we want to see God minister through us in the gifts of the Spirit, we must *spend time in the Word and in prayer with the Father.*

---

   c. When the disciples saw Him they cried out in fear **(verse 26)**. In this life there are many things that cause us to fear, but Jesus wants us to keep our focus on Him, not on the problems!

   d. Jesus responded to their fear, saying, **"Take courage!"** or in *The King James Version*, **"Be of good cheer!" verse 27**. Why allow fear, when we can have good cheer? We must replace the negative with the positive!

   e. Upon Peter's request, Jesus allowed him to participate in the miracle also. Do we "have not because we ask not"? (**James 4:2**)

f. Jesus' response to Peter's request was, **"Come" verse 29.** That is Jesus' response to us as well.

g. When Peter saw the wind, he became afraid. He cried out, **"Lord, save me!" verse 30.** Peter was overwhelmed by what he saw with his physical eyes, rather than believing Jesus. His faith was extinguished and fear overwhelmed him. Peter was in the middle of a miracle, but he took his attention off Jesus and began to sink. Are we any different?

h. When Peter began to sink, Jesus saved him (**verse 31**). Jesus never lets His disciples sink, despite our fears or momentary misgivings. We are never out of Jesus' sight.

i. Jesus connected faith in Him with miracles. In **John 10:37–38** He said, **"Do not believe me unless I do what my Father does. But if I do it, even though you do not believe me, believe the miracles, that you may know and understand that the Father is in me, and I in the Father."**

In **John 14:11–12** Jesus said, **"Believe me when I say that I am in the Father and the Father is in me; or at least believe on the evidence of the miracles themselves. I tell you the truth, anyone who has faith in me will do what I have been doing. He will do even greater things than these, because I am going to the Father."**

j. Miracles should be a part of our life! God encourages us to abide in Christ and to be available. As we trust and follow Him, He can demonstrate His love and power by performing miracles through us.

IV. Discussion of the Assigned Articles

ENCOURAGE THE DISCUSSION LEADER AND PARTICIPANTS TO FOCUS ON PORTIONS OF THE ARTICLE ASSIGNMENT THAT ARE IMPORTANT FOR THIS CLASS TO DISCUSS, ESPECIALLY AS IT RELATES TO THE MAIN PRINCIPLE.

V. Next Week's Assignment

A. REVIEW WITH THE CLASS NEXT WEEK'S ASSIGNMENT ON THE COURSE OUTLINE.

B. REVIEW THE MAIN PRINCIPLE FOR NEXT WEEK'S CLASS.

C. ASSIGN DISCUSSION LEADERS FOR LESSON 12: ONE PARTICIPANT TO LEAD THE BOOK DISCUSSION AND ANOTHER TO LEAD THE ASSIGNED ARTICLE DISCUSSION. FACILITATORS WILL LEAD THE DISCUSSION OF THE SCRIPTURES.

VI. Ministry Time

A. AS FACILITATOR YOU NEED TO GUIDE THE MINISTRY TIME.

Lesson 11 — Gifts of the Spirit—Power Gifts

B. IF YOU SENSE THE NEED FOR PERSONAL PRAYER MINISTRY IN A CLASS MEMBER, ASK THE PERSON CONCERNED IF HE WOULD LIKE PRAYER.

C. AT THE BEGINNING OF THE MINISTRY TIME, REMIND PARTICIPANTS ABOUT THE FOLLOWING:

As we minister to each other, we need to recognize that we are all fine-tuning our hearing of God's voice. We may not hear clearly all the time, so we need to carefully weigh any word of prophecy a class member gives us. The following is a helpful guideline:

If it doesn't make sense, put it on the shelf. If it contradicts what God has told you, let it drop. If your spirit confirms it, make a note of it in your journal and watch God bring it about.

D. PRAY THE FOLLOWING:

Lord, help us apply what we have learned by moving upon us with the **power gifts**—a gift of faith, gifts of healing or the working of miracles. We want the Holy Spirit to be free to operate through us. Reveal the operation of the Holy Spirit in these gifts, as He wills.

E. ENCOURAGE HANDS-ON MINISTRY BY CLASS MEMBERS. ALLOW THE GIFTS OF THE SPIRIT TO MANIFEST IN DIFFERENT PEOPLE.

F. BE CAREFUL THAT ONE PERSON DOES NOT DOMINATE THE MINISTERING.

G. CLOSE THE CLASS WITH PRAYER.

IN CHRIST

LESSON 12

GIFTS OF THE SPIRIT—VOCAL GIFTS

MAIN PRINCIPLE

When the Holy Spirit moves upon us with His vocal gifts, we can make evident God's specific word for our time and place.

WWW.ZOEMINISTRIES.ORG

LESSON 12

Gifts of the Spirit—Vocal Gifts

I. Let's Get Started!

   A. WELCOME THE CLASS.

   B. OPEN WITH PRAYER.

   C. WORSHIP THE LORD.

   D. READ, OR HAVE SOMEONE READ, THE MAIN PRINCIPLE FOR TODAY'S LESSON.

II. Supporting Principles From the Book

   ENCOURAGE THE DISCUSSION LEADER AND PARTICIPANTS TO FOCUS ON PORTIONS OF THE BOOK ASSIGNMENT THAT ARE IMPORTANT FOR THIS CLASS TO DISCUSS, ESPECIALLY AS IT RELATES TO THE MAIN PRINCIPLE.

III. Supporting Principles From Scripture—
   1 Corinthians 14
   Luke 2:25–35
   Acts 2:1–12
   Daniel 5

   A. 1 Corinthians 14

   1. In **chapter 14** there are several verses that mention the vocal gifts: the gift of prophesy, the gift of tongues and the interpretation of tongues.

2. The chapter begins and ends with a reference to the gift of prophecy. **Verse 1** includes the phrase **"eagerly desire spiritual gifts, especially the gift of prophecy." Verse 39** echoes this: **"Therefore, my brothers, be eager to prophesy, and do not forbid speaking in tongues."** The phrases **"eagerly desire"** and **"be eager"** are translated from the same Greek word, which can mean to desire earnestly, to envy and to be zealous in pursuit.[1] This is a passionate cry, encouraging us to ask God for words of prophecy!

3. **Verse 5** begins, **"I would like everyone of you to speak in tongues." Verse 18** says, **"I thank God that I speak in tongues more than all of you."** Paul makes it quite clear that the gift of tongues is one we should pursue.

4. **Verse 26** says, **"When you come together, everyone has a hymn, or a word of instruction, a revelation, a tongue or an interpretation. All of these must be done for the strengthening of the church."** The main goal of the vocal gifts is to strengthen the Church.

5. Paul encouraged the maintenance of order during a worship service (**verses 26–33**). He taught that the vocal gifts are always under the control of the speaker (**verse 32**). The Holy Spirit *empowers* but never *overpowers* us.

6. As the manifestation gifts are allowed to operate, the Holy Spirit brings freedom, edification and a desire to go deeper into the things of God.

We learn that God knows where we live—we understand that He knows us in a personal way.

7. Other verses in this chapter will be mentioned as we look at each of the vocal gifts.

B. The Gift of Prophecy

1. Definition of the *Gift of Prophecy:*

   HAVE SOMEONE READ THE DEFINITION FROM THE STUDY HELP **"THE VOCAL GIFTS."**

When the Holy Spirit moves through you with the gift of prophecy, you speak inspired words from the Lord. The message may foretell God's future plans or forthtell His perspective on the present, but it will come in response to human need.

John Dawson has described prophesying as follows:

> Many believers have been used by the Holy Spirit to impart a special word of encouragement to other believers in a prayer meeting or church service. When this occurs it is not a result of the Holy Spirit's grabbing the person and forcing speech from his lips. The person usually senses the beginning of what God wants to say and voluntarily yields to the Holy Spirit in expressing that thought. He begins in faith out of love for God and His people, and as thought follows thought the prophecy moves to completion.[2]

2. The Purpose of Prophecy

   a. **"But everyone who prophesies speaks to men for their strengthening, encouragement and comfort" 1 Corinthians 14:3.**

      - *Strengthening*— In the *King James Version* the word *edification* is used. In Greek the word to strengthen or edify is *oikodomeo* (oy-kod-om-eh´-o), which can mean to promote spiritual maturity and godly character.[3] Through prophecy the believer can be "built up."

      - *Encouragement*—This could also be translated as *exhortation*. To exhort is "to urge or incite by strong argument, advice or appeal; admonish earnestly."[4] Many times prophecies contain strong urging or earnest reproof or warning. Through prophecy the believer can be "stirred up."

      - *Comfort*—In Greek the word is *paramuthia* (par-am-oo-thee´-ah), which means to speak with someone in order to calm or console them.[5] Through prophecy the believer can be "lifted up."

   b. The Holy Spirit uses prophecy to convict and convince. **"But if an unbeliever or someone who does not understand comes in while everybody is prophesying, he will be convinced by all that he is a sinner and will be judged by all, and the secrets of his heart will be laid bare. So he will fall down and worship God, exclaiming, 'God is really among you!' " 1 Corinthians 14:24–25.**

c. The Holy Spirit can use prophecy to teach us. **"For you can all prophesy in turn so that everyone may be instructed and encouraged" 1 Corinthians 14:31.**

3. Prophecy should be judged by believers. **"Two or three prophets should speak, and the others should weigh carefully what is said" 1 Corinthians 14:29.**

4. Prophecy can be judged by the following:

   a. *The Word of God*—Most importantly, does it agree with Scripture? (**1 Corinthians 14:37**).

   b. *The witness of the Spirit*—Does the Holy Spirit inside of you agree? (**1 John 2:27**).

   c. *Testing the spirits*—What is the source of the prophecy? Are you dealing with an evil spirit? Are you dealing with a human spirit? Is this the Holy Spirit speaking? **"…Test the spirits to see whether they are from God, because many false prophets have gone out into the world" 1 John 4:1.** It is appropriate for the gift of discerning of spirits to be in operation as the vocal gifts are manifested.

   d. *The fruit*—Did the prophecy strengthen, encourage or comfort believers? (**1 Corinthians 14:3–4**).

   e. *Fulfillment of predictions*—Did it occur as predicted?

5. The Gift of Prophecy—**Luke 2:25–35**

Lesson 12 — Gifts of the Spirit—Vocal Gifts

a. The Holy Spirit was the source of the prophecy spoken by Simeon in this passage.

- **"The Holy Spirit was upon"** Simeon, who was devoted to God. The **"consolation of Israel"** refers to the comfort the Messiah would bring to His people.[6] Simeon was waiting in faith, patience and great longing for the coming of the Messiah (**verse 25**).

- **Verse 26 says, "It had been revealed to him by the Holy Spirit that he would not die before he had seen the Lord's Christ."** This may have been revealed to him through a word of knowledge.

- Simeon came into the temple courts because he was **"moved by the Spirit"** **verse 27**. His obedience led him to the Christ child, whom he recognized.

b. In **verses 29–32**, Simeon blessed God and prophesied. Luke, the author of this book and a Greek man himself, emphasized that Simeon's word of prophecy showed that salvation for **"all people"** meant that Gentiles, as well as the Jews, would be saved through Jesus.

c. **Verses 34–35** include a word of knowledge for Mary through Simeon. The gifts of the Spirit often flow together, so prophecy may contain words of knowledge or words of wisdom.

d. If someone gives you a personal prophecy, it

should bring confirmation of guidance that you have received from the Lord. If it does not make sense, lay it aside. If it is from God, He will bring it to pass in your life.

Prophecy should not be our guide; the Lord is our guide. Prophecy is meant to bring strength, encouragement and comfort.

C. The Gifts of Different Kinds of Tongues and Interpretation of Tongues

1. Definition of the *Gift of Different Kinds of Tongues:*

   HAVE SOMEONE READ THE DEFINITION FROM THE STUDY HELP **"THE VOCAL GIFTS."**

   The gift of different kinds of tongues is the ability to speak in a language one has not previously learned.[7]

   This gift is two-fold, either private or public. Paul referred to the private speaking in tongues in **1 Corinthians 14:14–15**. Here Paul implied that he often prayed or sang in tongues. The private speaking in tongues serves to edify the individual speaking (Jude 20). The public speaking in tongues serves to edify the church as the meaning of the message is interpreted (**1 Corinthians 14:5**).

   The gift of tongues includes the speaking of languages known to other people, as in **Acts 2:4–6**,

Lesson 12 — Gifts of the Spirit—Vocal Gifts

as well as the speaking of languages not known to other people, as in **1 Corinthians 13:1**.

2. Definition of *Interpretation of Tongues:*

HAVE SOMEONE READ THE DEFINITION FROM THE STUDY HELP **"THE VOCAL GIFTS."**

The gift of interpretation of tongues is "the Spirit-given ability to understand and communicate the meaning of an utterance spoken in tongues."[8]

a. There is a difference between interpreting and translating. To translate is to convert from one language to another. To interpret is to explain and unfold the meaning of something spoken. When an interpretation occurs there can be a valid difference between the length of the message given in tongues and the number of words required to express the meaning in the common language.

b. **"He who prophesies is greater than one who speaks in tongues, unless he interprets, so that the church may be edified" 1 Corinthians 14:5.** The goal is to edify believers (**1 Corinthians 14:12**). So, tongues spoken in public should be interpreted so that others may benefit from the message.

c. The gift of interpretation of tongues may be given to the one who speaks in tongues or to someone else.[9] Those who speak in tongues should pray for the gift of interpretation according to **1 Corinthians 14:13**.

d. **1 Corinthians 14:28 says, "If there is no interpreter, the speaker should keep quiet in the church and speak to himself and God."** If no one stands up to give the interpretation of what was spoken in tongues, then the person who spoke in tongues should stay yielded to the Lord and believe God will give him or her the interpretation.

3. The Purpose of Tongues and Interpretation of Tongues

   a. Like prophecy, tongues and interpretation of tongues serve to strengthen, encourage and comfort believers. Tongues with an interpretation are equal to prophecy in this respect (**1 Corinthians 14:3–6**).

   b. According to **1 Corinthians 14:22–25**, tongues can serve as a sign for the unbeliever.

An important purpose of the vocal gifts—prophecy and tongues with an interpretation—is to reveal the thoughts of the heart of the unbeliever so that he or she will recognize that God is real and present, and consequently bow down and worship Him.

---

   c. *Caution:* If everyone in a church speaks simultaneously in tongues, it can have the opposite effect. *The NIV Study Bible* footnote for **1 Corinthians 14:23** says, "The context is a meeting of the church in which everyone is speaking in tongues with the result that general confusion reigns…The visitors will be repulsed by the confusion, and the phenomenon meant to be an impressive sign will have a negative effect on the unsaved."[10]

d. When one person at a time speaks in tongues and the interpretation is given, people can be convicted or encouraged, and God is glorified.

4. The Gift of Tongues—**Acts 2:1–12**

   a. As the disciples were filled with the Holy Spirit they spoke with other tongues (**verse 4**).

   b. A crowd gathered as people from many nations heard the disciples speaking in their own respective languages (**verse 6**).

   c. The multi-ethnic crowd heard the disciples **"declaring the wonders of God"** in their own languages (**verse 11**).

   d. This is a dramatic illustration of the truth that speaking in tongues can be a sign for unbelievers (**1 Corinthians 14:22**).

   e. Phil and Rayma Schleppy, founders of Victory Ministries, shared a modern day example of this.

   The Schleppys were ministering in a Colorado prison. The room was filled to capacity, with several inmates sitting along the walls. The

Lord gave Rayma a message in tongues and then the interpretation. Rayma recalls that the interpretation she was given was for the whole group.

After the meeting, a young man came up to Rayma and asked, "Are you Indian? Sioux Indian?"

Rayma replied, "No, I'm not Indian at all!"

The young man said, "But you spoke in a Sioux dialect! God gave you a message just for me. When I heard it, I started praying, and I got my heart right with God!"

5. The Gift of Interpretation of Tongues—**Daniel 5**

   a. During a banquet, a hand appeared and wrote a message on the wall facing King Belshazzar (**verse 5**).

   b. The writing was in a language unknown to those at the banquet. The king summoned wise men and astrologers, but they could not read the writing or interpret its meaning (**verses 7–8**).

   c. Daniel was able to give the interpretation because, as the queen said, he had **"the spirit of the holy gods in him** [actually, the Spirit of the One True God]" (**verse 11**).

   d. *Dake's Annotated Reference Bible* states, "The writing could not be understood until interpreted by Daniel. To teach that the original writing was in Chaldee, Hebrew, Samaritan or any known language of the Babylonian Empire is to propagate fallacy, for if this had been the case some of the lords from all over the empire could have interpreted it without the divine help through Daniel. There is no indication that he could read it by his own natural ability. As to the words being in Chaldee they are translations of the original words in some unknown language."[11]

e. The interpretation that Daniel received and spoke carried a message of severe correction from the God Most High. The predicted events took place that very evening (**verses 30–31**).

D. Closing Thoughts

1. As we conclude this course on the Holy Spirit, we should remember that the best way to operate in the spiritual gifts is to **"follow the way of love" 1 Corinthians 14:1.** It is a shame when we see people being "beat up" through the harsh use of prophecy. Each word of prophecy needs to be imparted with love—without condemnation. When we minister in the love that the Lord desires, we will see God's manifested presence in our midst.

2. Let us also be reminded that it is the Giver of all good gifts on whom we want to focus our attention. The following quote comes from John Rea's book, *The Holy Spirit in the Bible:*

> The Spirit is God pouring Himself out as water to revive parched souls and to supply the vitalizing power that transforms lives (Isaiah 32:15; 44:3; John 7:38) and floods them with joy (Acts 13:52; Rom. 14:17; 15:13; 1 Thess. 1:5-6).

He is the Eternal Spirit, the Spirit of Yahweh, the Spirit of Christ, the promised Holy Spirit who was sent forth at Pentecost to empower the church. *It is God's will that He, the third Person of the Trinity, be with you and in you and upon you* both now and forever. Amen. [emphasis added][12]

3. Like Abraham, we are blessed so that we can be a blessing to all nations (**Galatians 3:8–9**). The overall purpose of the gifts of the Spirit is to enable us to be a blessing to the body of Christ and to unbelievers.

IV. Discussion of the Assigned Articles

ENCOURAGE THE DISCUSSION LEADER AND PARTICIPANTS TO FOCUS ON PORTIONS OF THE ARTICLE ASSIGNMENT THAT ARE IMPORTANT FOR THIS CLASS TO DISCUSS, ESPECIALLY AS IT RELATES TO THE MAIN PRINCIPLE.

V. Ministry Time

A. AS FACILITATOR YOU NEED TO GUIDE THE MINISTRY TIME.

B. IF YOU SENSE THE NEED FOR PERSONAL PRAYER MINISTRY IN A CLASS MEMBER, ASK THE PERSON CONCERNED IF HE WOULD LIKE PRAYER.

C. AT THE BEGINNING OF THE MINISTRY TIME, REMIND PARTICIPANTS ABOUT THE FOLLOWING:

As we minister to each other, we need to recognize that we are all fine-tuning our hearing of God's voice. We may not hear clearly all the time, so we need to carefully weigh any word of prophecy a class member gives us. The following is a helpful guideline:

If it doesn't make sense, put it on the shelf. If it contradicts what God has told you, let it drop. If your spirit confirms it, make a note of it in your journal and watch God bring it about.

D. PRAY THE FOLLOWING:
Lord, help us apply what we have learned by moving upon us with the **vocal gifts**—a gift of prophecy, a gift of speaking in different tongues or a gift of interpretation of tongues. We want the Holy Spirit to be free to operate through us. Reveal the operation of the Holy Spirit in these gifts, as He wills.

E. ENCOURAGE HANDS-ON MINISTRY BY CLASS MEMBERS. ALLOW THE GIFTS OF THE SPIRIT TO MANIFEST IN DIFFERENT PEOPLE.

F. BE CAREFUL THAT ONE PERSON DOES NOT DOMINATE THE MINISTERING.

G. CLOSE WITH PRAYER.

VI. Ending Notes to Facilitators

IF CLASS MEMBERS EXPRESS AN INTEREST IN TAKING ANOTHER ZOE TRAINING COURSE, CONTACT A ZOE REPRESENTATIVE. A LIST OF ZOE COURSE DESCRIPTIONS IS IN THE LESSON

12 SECTION OF THE *IN CHRIST STUDY GUIDE*. ENCOURAGE PARTICIPANTS TO READ ABOUT OUR COURSES ON THE ZOE WEBSITE AT: WWW.ZOEMINISTRIES.ORG/ZOE-COURSES

ENDNOTES

Scripture quotations appear from the following versions:
Holy Bible, New International Version, Zondervan Bible Publishers, Grand Rapids, Michigan, 1988.
The Message, Eugene H. Peterson, Colorado Springs, Colorado: NavPress Publishing Group, 1993.
King James Version, Cleveland, Ohio: The World Publishing Co.
The Amplified Bible, Grand Rapids, Michigan: Zondervan Publishing House, 1987.
The Spirit Filled Life Bible—New King James Version, Nashville, Tennesee: Thomas Nelson Publishers, 1991.
Life Application Bible—The Living Bible, Wheaton, Illinois: Tyndale House Publishers, Inc. and Youth for Christ USA, 1988.

Scripture quotations are from the *New International Version* unless otherwise noted.

Lesson 1

1. [be] *The NIV Study Bible* (Grand Rapids, Michigan: Zondervan Publishing House, 1985), p. 1630, footnote 17:11.

2. [glory] Joseph H. Thayer, *Thayer's Greek-English Lexicon of the New Testament* (Grand Rapids, Michigan: Baker Book House, 1977), p.156, #1391.

3. [vessel] George Ricker Berry, *Interlinear Greek-English New Testament* (Grand Rapids, Michigan: Baker Book House, 1981), p. 4636.

4. [concealed treasure] *The NIV Study Bible*, p. 1767, footnote 4:7.

ENDNOTES

5. [light in heart] Ibid., p. 1767, footnote 4:6.

Lesson 2

1. [spiritual unity] *The Full Life Study Bible* (Springfield, Missouri: Life Publishers International, 1992), p. 1829, footnote 4:3.

2. [true vine] *The NIV Study Bible*, p. 1626, footnote 15:1.

3. [fruit] Ibid., footnote 15:2.

4. [pruning] John Gretti, *Grape Pruning for the Home Garden* (Golden, Colorado: Cooperative Extension Service, Colorado State University), p. 7.

5. [fruit production] Ibid., p. 7.

6. [abide] Thayer, p. 399, #3306.

Lesson 3

1. [living sacrifice] *The NIV Study Bible*, p. 1725.

2. [transform] Thayer, p.405, #3339

3. [need/needle] Chuck Swindoll, title unknown.

4. [propheteia] James Strong, *Strong's Exhaustive Concordance of the Bible* (Nashville, Tennessee: Crusade Bible Publishers, Inc., 1990), #4394 and #4396.

5. [perception motive gift] Marvin R. Vincent, D.D., *Vincent's Word Studies of the New Testament*, Volume 3 (McClean, Virginia: MacDonald Publishing Company), p. 156.

6. [diakonia] Strong, #1248.

7. [serving] Vincent, p. 157.

Lesson 4

1. [perception MG] Don and Katie Fortune, *Discover Your God Given Gifts* (Grand Rapids, Michigan: Chosen Books, 1987), pp. 72–74.

2. [serving MG] Ibid., pp. 95–96.

3. [understanding] Vincent, p. 157.

4. [didasko] Strong, #1321.

5. [paraklesis] Ibid., # 3874.

6. [aims at will/heart] Vincent, p. 157.

Lesson 5

1. [perception MG] Vincent, p. 156.

2. [teaching MG] Fortune, p. 115.

3. [exhortation MG] Ibid., p. 136.

4. [giving MG] Ibid., p. 138.

5. [metadidomi] Strong, #3330.

6. [haplotetes] Fortune, p. 138.

7. [giver] Vincent, p. 157.

8. [proistemi] Strong, #4291.

9. [administrator] Vincent, p. 158.

Lesson 6

1. [giving MG] Fortune, pp. 157–158.

2. [administration MG] Ibid., pp. 179–180.

3. [eleeo] Strong, #1653.

4. [mercy with joy] Kenneth S. Wuest, *The New Testament—An Expanded Translation* (Iowa Falls, Iowa: Riverside Book and Bible House, 1984), p. 373.

Lesson 7

1. [compassion MG] Fortune, pp. 200–201.

Lesson 8

1. [greatest unused power] Paul Lee Tan, Th.D., *Encyclopedia of 7700 Illustrations* (Dallas, Texas: Bible Communications, 1979), p. 555, #2232

2. [Elohim] Arthur, p. 21.

3. [brood] Strong, #7363.

Lesson 9

1. [live] Kenneth S. Wuest, *Wuest Word Studies From the Greek New Testament* (Grand Rapids, Michigan: William B. Eerdmans Publishing Co., 1972), Galatians p. 162

2. [stoicheo] Strong, #4748.

3. [Moody] *1,100 Illustrations From the Writings of D.L. Moody* (Grand Rapids, Michigan: Baker Books, 1996), p. 147.

4. [bara] Bob Yandian, *One Flesh* (Tulsa, Oklahoma: Pillar Books and Publishing, 1992), p. 4.

5. [Elohim] Kay Arthur, *Lord, I Want to Know You* (Colorado Springs, Colorado: WaterBrook Press, 1992), p. 9.

6. [ruwach] Strong, #7307.

7. [brood] Strong, #7363.

8. [Yahweh] Arthur, pp. 55-56.

9. [painting] Tan, p.205, #489.

10. [parakletos] Strong, #3875.

11. [dove's vision] Watchman Nee, *Song of Songs* (Fort Washington, Pennsylvania: Christian Literature Crusade, 1965), p. 33.

Lesson 10

1. [word of wisdom] Dick Iverson, *The Holy Spirit Today* (Portland, Oregon: Bible Temple Publishing, 1976), p. 104.

2. [integrity] Finis Jennings Dake, *Dake's Annotated Reference Bible* (Lawrenceville, Georgia: Dake Bible Sales, Inc., 1963), p. 24, column 4, note i.

3. [truth] Ibid.

4. [hupokrites] Thayer, p. 643, #5273 and William Morris, Ed., *The American Heritage Dictionary of the English Language*

ENDNOTES

(Boston, Massachusetts: American Heritage Publishing Co., Inc. and Houghton Mifflin Company, 1969), p. 381.

5. [word of knowledge] Iverson, pp. 114–115.

6. [discerning of spirits] Ibid., p. 123.

7. [sorcerer] *The Full Life Study Bible*, p. 1675, footnote 13:8.

8. [opposed] Thayer, p. 45, #436.

9. [believe] Strong, #4100.

Lesson 11

1. [gift of faith] *The Full Life Study Bible*, p. 1770.

2. [no rain] *The NIV Study Bible*, p. 509, footnote 17:1.

3. [rapha] Gesenius, pp. 775-776, #7495.

4. [marpe] Ibid., pp. 510-511, #4832.

5. [therapeuo] Strong, #2323.

6. [sozo] Strong, #4982.

7. [iaomai] Thayer, p. 296, #2392.

8. [miracles] *The Full Life Study Bible*, p. 1771.

9. [miracle] Iverson, p. 147.

10. [dunamis] Strong, #1411.

Lesson 12

1. [eagerly desire] Thayer, p. 271, #2206.

2. [prophecy] John Dawson, exact source unknown.

3. [strengthen] *The Full Life Study Bible*, p. 1776, footnote 14:26.

4. [exhort] *The American Heritage Dictionary of the English Language*, p. 460.

5. [paramuthia] Thayer, p. 485, #3889.

6. [consolation of Israel] *The NIV Study Bible*, p. 1539, footnote 2:25.

7. [tongues] Ibid., p. 1645, footnote 2:4.

8. [interpretation of tongues] *The Full Life Study Bible*, p. 1771.

9. [interpretation given] Ibid., p. 1771.

10. [not all at once] *The NIV Study Bible*, p. 1754, footnote 14:23.

11. [Daniel interprets] Dake, p. 862, column 4, note q.

12. [Spirit of God] John Rea, *The Holy Spirit in the Bible* (Lake Mary, Florida: Creation House, Strange Communications Co., 1990), p. 350.

APPENDIX A

Guidelines for a Personal Visit/Phone Call with Discussion Leaders

1. **Before the visit:**

   a. Set up a time to visit/call the couple/class member and tell them what the purpose of the visit/call is.

   b. Ask God what He wants to do in this couple/class member so that you will know how to pray for them personally. Ask for His guidance and protection during your time with the leaders.

   c. Look at the class material so that you will be able to answer any questions they have regarding the book, article and Scripture assignments.

2. **During the visit/call:**

   a. Pray that God would bless your time together and that He would bring to mind those things that need to be discussed.

   b. Ask how they are doing. Ask if they are enjoying the course.

   c. Ask if they have read the article with "Guidelines for Leading a Class Discussion." Ask if they have any questions about this.

   d. Ask them if they have any questions about the information in the book, article or Scripture assignments. Ask if the Holy Spirit has given them any new insights.

CONT'D APPENDIX A

    e. Ask if they have questions to stimulate discussion related to the Main Principle.

    f.. Encourage them to be open to the Holy Spirit's leading as they prepare and lead the class.

    g. Pray together and ask the Lord to anoint them for this task.

3. **After the visit:**

    a. Pray for God's anointing, guidance and protection of these participants as they serve as discussion leaders.

    b. Pray that God would continue to work in their lives.

APPENDIX B

Holy Spirit Scriptures

1. Promised Holy Spirit
   a. John 14:15-19, 25-27
   b. Mark 1:6-8
   c. Acts 1:4, 5, 8
   d. Luke 24:46-49

2. Being Filled
   a. Acts 1-4
   b. Acts 10:36-48
   c. Acts 19:1-7

3. Purpose
   a. Worship/blessings - 1 Corinthians 14:14, 15a
   b. Praying in our innermost being - Romans 8:26b-28
   c. Building up our faith - Jude 20
   d. Part of the Armor - Ephesians 6:18

4. Is This For Today?
   Hebrews 13:8

5. Preparation for Prayer/Prayer
   Luke 11:9-13

6. Follow-Up
   a. John 10:10 and Mark 1:8
   b. Phone calls or visits
   c. Have disciple read book of Acts

www.ingramcontent.com/pod-product-compliance
Lightning Source LLC
Chambersburg PA
CBHW051049160426
43193CB00010B/1122